INNOVATIONS IN
HIGHER EDUCATION

Part of the American Council on Education, Series on Higher Education
Susan Slesinger, Executive Editor

Other titles in the series:

Fitting Form to Function: A Primer on the Organization of Academic Institutions
by Rudolph H. Weingartner

Learning to Lead: A Handbook for Postsecondary Administrators
by James R. Davis

The "How To" Grants Manual: Successful Grantseeking Techniques for Obtaining Public and Private Grants
Seventh Edition by David G. Bauer

Leading from the Middle: A Case-Study Approach to Academic Leadership for Associate Deans
by Tammy Stone and Mary Coussons-Read

Higher Education Assessments: Leadership Matters
by Gary L. Kramer and Randy L. Swing

Leading the Campaign: Advancing Colleges and Universities
by Michael J. Worth

Leaders in the Labyrinth: College Presidents and the Battlegrounds of Creeds and Convictions
by Stephen J. Nelson

Academic Turnarounds: Restoring Vitality to Challenged American Colleges/Universities
Edited by Terrence MacTaggart

Managing Diversity Flashpoints in Higher Education
by Joseph E. Garcia and Karen J. Hoelscher

Leaders in the Crossroads: Success and Failure in the College Presidency
by Stephen James Nelson

International Students: Strengthening a Critical Resource
Edited by Maureen S. Andrade and Norman W. Evans

Faculty Success through Mentoring: A Guide for Mentors, Mentees, and Leaders by Carole J. Bland, Anne L. Taylor, S. Lynn Shollen, Anne Marie Weber-Main, Patricia A. Mulcahy

Leading America's Branch Campuses edited by Samuel Schuman

Beyond 2020: Envisioning the Future of Universities in America
by Mary Landon Darden

Out in Front: The College President as the Face of the Institution
edited by Lawrence V. Weill

Community Colleges on the Horizon: Challenge, Choice, or Abundance
Edited by Richard Alfred, Christopher Shults, Ozan Jaquette, and Shelley Strickland

Minding the Dream: The Process and Practice of the American Community College by Gail O. Mellow and Cynthia Heelan

INNOVATIONS IN HIGHER EDUCATION

Igniting the Spark for Success

**Allan M. Hoffman
and Stephen D. Spangehl**

AMERICAN COUNCIL ON EDUCATION
The Unifying Voice for Higher Education

ROWMAN & LITTLEFIELD PUBLISHERS, INC.
Lanham • Boulder • New York • Toronto • Plymouth, UK

Published by Rowman & Littlefield Publishers, Inc.
A wholly owned subsidary of The Rowman & Littlefield Publishing Group,
Inc.
4501 Forbes Boulevard, Suite 200, Lanham, Maryland 20706
http://www.rowmanlittlefield.com

Estover Road, Plymouth PL6 7PY, United Kingdom

British Library Cataloguing in Publication Information Available

Library of Congress Cataloging-in-Publication Data

Hoffman, Allan M. (Allan Michael)
 Innovations in higher education : igniting the spark for success / Allan M.
Hoffman and Stephen D. Spangehl.
 p. cm.
"Published in partnership with the American Council on Education."
 ISBN 978-1-4422-0446-1 (cloth : alk. paper) — ISBN 978-1-4422-0448-5
(electronic)
 1. Education, Higher—United States. 2. Educational innovations--United
States.
 3. Educational change—United States. 4.
LA227.4 .H63 2012
 158—dc23   2011021353

∞™ The paper used in this publication meets the minimum requirements of
American National Standard for Information Sciences—Permanence of Paper
for Printed Library Materials, ANSI/NISO Z39.48-1992.

Printed in the United States of America

CONTENTS

LIST OF FIGURES

ACKNOWLEDGMENTS

I am fortunate in that I worked with an exceptionally talented and gifted friend and colleague, John Holzhüter of Ottawa, Kansas. John assisted with the research and writing of this book; he spent countless hours turning abstracts, notes, and conversations into paragraphs and chapters. As senior volume editor, I feel his work was crucial to the production of this book. His critical wisdom and creativity is clearly embedded in each page. John exemplifies the true meaning of *friend*, and as a practicing minister, he is the embodiment of the intersection of the kind, caring Samaritan. I also want to extend my thanks and gratitude to Trish Dowd Kelne for her extraordinary editorial work. John and Trish are very special people; thank you.

I also owe a debt of gratitude to volume coeditor Dr. Stephen Spangehl. Our numerous conversations and combined research proving that American higher education is both innovative and responsive is the basis of this book. Our frequent and detailed debates and discussions became the impetus and stimulus for this volume. His work with the Academic Quality Improvement Program of the Higher Learning Commission places Steve in a unique role to interact with the best practitioners of higher education. Steve always had just one more case study, one more idea, and one more perspective about how we could add to this volume.

Susan Slesinger, senior editor, is especially acknowledged. Susan worked tirelessly helping with this book from abstract to concrete.

A special thanks to my wife Annie for her faith, love, and encouragement. Without her, the world is abstract. I also want to acknowledge my children and grandchildren. Emily, Elijah and Benjamin; Andrew and Elizabeth; Heather and Dr. Brent; Allie and Cody, for they have taught me the meaning of life and the value of innovation.

Finally to the men and women of American higher education: Please know your efforts matter greatly. In the words of Sir Winston Churchill, statesman, war hero, philosopher, "Never, never, never give up." Believe you change lives. Know you make a difference.

Allan M. Hoffman

PREFACE

It is eleven years into the new millennium, and the landscape of higher education in the United States remains mercurial. Students and funders are expecting prolific, tangible evidence of success and demanding greater levels of accountability and transparency in for-profit, state-sponsored, and not-for-profit institutions. Curricular reforms, technological advances, and the globalization of social and intellectual perspectives are propelling innovative approaches and strategic reform in all aspects of the higher education system. While this helps to address earlier concerns of accessibility and diversity, it also mandates a constant evolution in research and delivery. Additionally, improvements in the structure, tools, and processes of higher education in this country tend to move at a pace that trails international counterparts. National completion forces administrators to balance increased fiscal and marketing pressures with external accreditation requirements and federal scrutiny. The "industry" of education continues to lag behind its global competitors. The United States ranks in the bottom half (sixteenth out of the twenty-seven countries examined) in the proportion of students who complete a college degree or certificate program. According to the National Center for Public Policy and Higher Education (2006), "The current level of performance [in

U.S. higher education] will fall short in a world being reshaped by the knowledge-based global economy" (p. 5).

Even more problematic, the increasing costs of higher education have continued to outpace inflation at a critical time of national fiscal concern. As cited in Margaret Spellings's report,

> While students bear the immediate brunt of tuition increases, affordability is also a crucial policy dilemma for those who are asked to fund higher education, notably federal and state taxpayers. Even as institutional costs go up, state subsidies are decreasing and public concern about affordability may eventually contribute to an erosion of confidence in higher education. In our view, affordability is directly affected by a financing system that provides limited incentives for colleges and universities to take aggressive steps to improve institutional efficiency and productivity. (Spellings, 2006, p. 2)

This rhetoric, combined with deep state and federal budget cuts and a general social and political impatience, has revived calls for reform in educational affordability, curriculum, and outcome measurement. When a critical mass of stakeholders is sufficiently motivated to anticipate change in an institution, a slow response can threaten the survival of the organization. Retrospectively, we know that when an institution fails to gain the widespread perception of rapid improvement, then the institution's opportunity to continue the internal process of "educational innovation" may be lost. This loss is soon supplanted by the demand for the external process of "educational reform." *Educational reform* is a plan, program, or movement that attempts to bring about a change in educational theory or practice. Typically, "educational reform" refers to a broad plan of systemic change across a community or society. In contrast, "*innovation* is the sequence of activities by which a new element is introduced into a social unit, with the intention of benefiting the unit, some part of it, or the wider society. The element need not to be entirely novel or unfamiliar to members of the unit, but it must involve some discernible change or challenge of the status quo" (West and Farr, 1990, p. 9).

The status quo of higher education is in question today. Expectations are once again demanding new approaches and strategic improvement in all aspects of the higher education system. While a strong

and system-wide commitment to change exists (and some global com-
monalties are notable), no "universal strategies" apply to institutional
particularities and contexts. However, within such an environment, a
myriad of success stories are being forged from educational institutions, supporting industries, and educational consortiums that choose to
traverse the monumental complexity of "innovation." It is the intention
of this book to bring higher education professionals together as part
of a broad, national movement to encourage such dynamic effort, to
motivate reflection at the precipice, and to promote fresh ideas as part
of the ongoing work. We hope to fuel institutional sharing through the
illustration of successful pilot programming and the documentation of
tools proven to maximize efficiencies crucial to the continued success of
the entire higher learning community. In the chapters that follow, we
have the privilege of presenting innovative illustrations, submitted from
practitioners at a variety of tertiary institutions. These works are the
result of a tremendous response to our call for submissions from innovators in the field. The final selections were chosen based on their merit,
originality, and testimony of success. We are extremely grateful to all of
the contributors and their supporting organizations.

                                                                        Allan M. Hoffman

I

A VIEW FROM THE TOP

Allan M. Hoffman
John Holzhüter

In the decade before the "educational reform movement" of the 1980s, the administration of Richard Nixon proposed the creation of a Foundation for Higher Education based on the recommendations of the Carnegie Commission (Carnegie Foundation for the Advancement of Teaching, 1968). In 1972, $10 million was allocated by congress in the budget of the Department of Health, Education, and Welfare to "improve higher education" in response to the growing demand to reshape educational theories and practices. It was a clear evolution to more inclusive and holistic views on the primary purposes of postsecondary learning. Discussion around institutions of higher education began to more frequently group the previously isolated institutions of junior and community colleges, trade and vocational schools, and both private and state-sponsored universities. There was a general softening in the prevalent national view that a four-year degree was universally the most effective assurance of life success. As the one-size-fits-all approach to tertiary learning came into question, the concept of "universal access to education" began to be viewed as an individualized means of personal fulfillment. Increasing discussion arose on the scope and importance of curriculums that extended beyond mere technical or practical proficiencies. Efforts to equip students to collectively promote social justice and individually impact social change began to extend beyond colleges and universities to all institutions of higher learning. Continuing education was becoming viewed as a pathway to expand self-efficacy, improve quality of life, and encourage social connection and civic responsibility. In this context, the concept of innovation was essentially a process of systemic improvement(s).

Under the Reagan administration, a dramatic priority shift came about in both the sociopolitical expectations and the federally scrutinized objectives of higher education. Such a shift gave voice to calls for uniform curriculums with an emphasis on "performance mastery." Uniform standards of test-indicated competencies were encouraged among like institutions, and participation in higher education was connected with job readiness and linked with international competiveness and national, economic goals. Students with "high scores" were expected to compete for additional educational opportunities and ultimately the best jobs in their respective fields. In this climate, the concept of innovation was essentially a means of creating better educational "products," better-prepared and higher-competency-scoring graduates.

In the years since, these competing and sometimes conflicting views on the role and goals of higher education have continued to challenge and confound administrators, regulators, and academics alike. The place and focus of community colleges, the role of shareholders in for-profit institutions, and the practicality of student-sharing partnerships among different types of tertiary institutions continue to be the subject of both scrutiny and prototype. In the following chapters, we look back on the evolution of the higher education system, examine current views on accreditation and student measurement, and explore the perspectives of university and community college leaders on institutional identity and challenges facing higher education.

THE EVOLUTION OF HIGHER EDUCATION

Innovation as Natural Selection
Allan M. Hoffman and John Holzhüter

"We must take change by the hand or rest assuredly, change will take us by the throat."

—Winston Churchill

Innovation resembles mutation, the biological process that keeps species evolving so they can better compete for survival. As we look closely at how innovation works in practice, we see that it is most effective when institutions honestly identify the environmental pressures they face and aggressively search for the niches in which they can effectively compete. Just as successful species over-reproduce, increasing the chances that a random mutation will turn out to be advantageous, successful innovative organizations promote the generation of many ideas, selecting only the most promising for further development. Imagining and implementing new ideas is only half of innovation. The other half, as with evolution, involves the ruthless testing of whether a change actually constitutes an advancement, an improvement over the process and activities it replaced.

While evolution makes this testing a matter of survival, ensuring that only the advantageous changes can persist, innovations must be measured and tested impartially and unemotionally. It is a sobering fact that the new can often seem more attractive than the familiar, that without the rigor of metrics and disinterested observation, we are all liable to the corollaries of the Hawthorne Effect (Landsberger, 1955), so sucked along in our enthusiasm for what we have invented that we defend it regardless of its actual merits. As natural selection retains in the gene pool only those traits that actually aid survival, so, too, innovators must be willing to adjust underperforming innovations and discard those that fail to live up to their promise. In the battle to survive in a rapidly changing educational environment, institutions that innovate have a strong natural advantage. GE's Jack Welch warns that "if the rate of change inside an organization is less than the rate of change outside, the end is in sight."

THE GERMINATION OF ACADEMIC INNOVATION

Higher learning has historically been slow to adopt the realities of this natural selection process. It tended instead to follow an "internally directed" approach more resembling the proposition of intelligent design. This was built and reinforced by the origins of the institutions themselves. Through the early twentieth century, organizations of higher education were largely created and fostered by religious or community groups or training extensions for military cadets. While there was the tiny glimmer of federal and state involvement, there was little focus on access or tangible outcomes. Curricular improvements were largely driven by the intense rivalries within the system. Faith-based schools, grown through denominational support, recognized imperatively that their success was a reflective component in the prestige and growth of faith-based sponsors. Local institutions and the communities they occupied understood that the bragging rights and employment opportunities afforded could attract residents to their towns.

Marketing strategies touted reputations built on promulgated institutional achievements or the recognition of niche-based successes. Still, it was through a predictable classical study curriculum that similar student pools nationwide were targeted and trained. Outcomes were primarily gauged through student completion and mastery standards, which varied widely from school to school. By and large, overall institutional accomplishment was illustrated through growth in enrollment and expansions in programming. Student attendance, in-class interactions, and "the essay" were the prime contributors to assured commencement. A handshake at the proscenium and award of a diploma were the only tangible validations of success expected from students specifically and society in general. A new dimension of competition was introduced with the creation of publicly funded land-grant institutions in the mid-1800s.

Sanctioned to ensure that the United States remained competitive in the wake of the industrial revolution, these schools competed to churn out graduates with practical skills in the areas of agriculture, science, and engineering. The burden to develop new educational products fell to entrenched experts in the field. Rivalry and world events drove innovative practices within a closed system. The business of education remained internally led and safely ensconced in its hierarchies. With the national entry into and the aftermath of the First World War, the United States clearly led the world in industry-supportive innovations. Higher learning led the way in the introduction of new ideas and new applications, albeit through necessity. Curriculums rapidly morphed, evolved, and specialized. Through timely adaptation, higher education had survived any scrutiny of its merit or questions of its effectiveness. National pride and confidence in the value of instruction was reinforced through the winning of the war and continuing successes of the American business, science, and industry sectors. The stock market crash of October 1929 brought new challenges to the entire educational system.

The Great Depression caused funding reductions that greatly impacted the quality of primary and secondary education. From 1929 to 1932, school year durations were shortened, some by more than ten days (U.S. Office of Education, 1938). Liberal arts and college preparatory courses were cut, and classrooms became overcrowded. There was immense pressure to graduate students from high school who otherwise may have been retained. The higher education system, with encouragement from the government, responded with the growth and widespread utilization of junior colleges. Originally launched in Chicago in 1901 to focus on freshman and sophomore instruction in an attempt to free up university resources and serve as screening centers for intellectual elite (Brint and Karabel, 1989), the concept was initially slow to spread. By 1920, there were fifty-two junior colleges in the nation, ten of which were publicly funded. By 1928, there were 248 two-year colleges, nearly half of which were public. These became viable options for students with limited funds or those not adequately prepared for college instruction.

Junior college enrollment in 1928 was close to 45,000 students (Brint and Karabel, 1989). At the same time, the percentage of high school graduates attending college in the year after their graduation had started to drop from 31.5 percent in 1929 to 22.9 percent in 1933 (U.S. Office of Education, 1935). Enrollment at four-year colleges went into decline, falling 8.6 percent from 1932 to 1934 (U.S. Office of Education, 1935). While the overall system was changing to meet the needs of the consumer, a widening gap had formed. In addition to being segregated by race and gender, students were becoming involuntarily sorted along the lines of income, location, and academic preparation. While decreasing enrollments presented a threat to four-year institutions, there was little momentum to expand their acceptance criteria, modify their cost structures, or bolster remedial curriculums. Higher education, while potentially dynamic and inventive, remained stymied by hierarchical constant. This time, external pressure toward innovations was viewed as something to rally against, not rush to embrace.

By and large, college leaders felt adaptations solely to meet current social demand would erode institutional effectiveness and reputation. Internal debates or calls to adapt to changing student requirements were muted, often through the sheer personality of institutional leaders. As public needs were being met through the system at large, there was no social outcry. The general consensus was that tertiary education could best discern its own business needs. The educational system began to primarily evolve through a process of insular mutations.

AFTER TEN YEARS OF DEPRESSION
AND FIVE YEARS OF WAR . . .

By the middle of the twentieth century, higher education had again become more responsive to external demands for adaptation, transformation, and change. Attendance declines experienced during the Second World War were exponentially rectified with the implementation of the Servicemen's Readjustment Act of 1944, more commonly known as the GI Bill of Rights. Federal assurances of direct tuition payments to colleges, trade schools, and business and agricultural training programs infused immediate capital. There were huge boosts in student enrollment. By 1947, federal resources reported that veterans made up 49 percent of college attendees. By the time the original GI Bill ended in July 1956, 7.8 million World War II veterans had utilized educational benefits. Gains in student quantity were mirrored by dynamic increases in the college preparedness levels of new enrollees. This new student element had practical training and hands-on experience with innovative technologies. They had many preexisting skills preferred by employers and assured access to federal funds to start their own businesses. With the temporary postponement of attendance and fiscal concerns came opportunities to focus on additional stakeholder needs.

With innovative practices often mandated, widely practiced, and peer-taught by the business sector, institutions started to explore peacetime partnership opportunities. Industries sought out academic partners to assist with cutting-edge research and development projects spawned by new technologies. In the postwar years from 1948 to 1973, economists estimate that two thirds of U.S. economic growth was driven by education and the innovation it produced (Carnevale and Desrochers, 2002). Unfortunately, a decade later, meeting the ongoing responsiveness expectations of these new business partners was proving increasingly difficult. By the early 1960s, it was becoming apparent that the needs of business and industry were beginning to outpace academic delivery speed. It was neither insular ignorance nor philosophical apathy that mired rapid institutional response, merely a scramble to reprioritize.

Administrators were facing increasingly vocal student concerns and the mounting effects of social upheaval. Individual educators who fought to champion innovative initiatives were leaving academia for more lucrative jobs in the private sector. Overall, systems of higher education were compelled to bridle rapid institutional change in an effort to maintain student control and mitigate campus chaos. For many schools, the more immediate crisis of desegregation compliance and the federal scrutiny it presented shifted their remaining focus from academic responsiveness. While most of the colleges and schools desegregated without direct federal intervention or defiant governors, recruiting of minority students was focused on candidates who were "smart and well adjusted." This approach was soon applied to non-minority student recruitment as well.

The brighter the members of the student pool, the more potentially successful the career of the graduates. It was a win-win for the business of education, potentially increasing effective outcomes with minimal changes to existing delivery systems. There was no longer the pressing need to focus on improving learning standards or maximizing the effectiveness of teaching methodologies. With interest at record highs and limited classroom and resource availability, the "privilege" of tertiary education once again became an opportunity bestowed on serious, well-prepared students or those with access to financial resources. Higher education was no longer in the mood to innovate. This was the status quo as the baby boomers showed up at college campuses and the federal government began to target efforts expanding educational opportunities.

DEMANDS FOR A PARADIGM SHIFT

The Economic Opportunity Act of 1964 provided tutoring, mentoring, and other assistance to low-income, first-generation college students to increase their retention and graduation rates (now known as TRIO programs). The passage of the Higher Education Act of 1965 assured that every student who wanted to enroll in college could afford to do so. Higher education was facing the looming reality of permanent federal involvement and the emergence of a new political emphasis on the "public right to successful higher education." Not surprisingly, enrollment at public institutions ballooned first, followed by increased applications at private institutions of higher education. This new student population brought learning-style, economic, and social-integration challenges incompatible with the existing campus culture. Governmental scrutiny and the expectations of the newly enrolled demanded innovations that could assure that a continuum of diverse learning needs would be met. Schools slow to improve were met with both federal mandates and student hostility.

Three years later, low-income and first-generational students continued to face a myriad of financial, scholarly, and social challenges in the halls of higher education. Federal involvement expanded with the first reauthorization of the Higher Education Act in 1968, which created additional student resource requirements through the Student Support Services Program. Demand for higher education continued to escalate with the emergence of the "nontraditional" student. While some older students enrolled as federal subsidies now made continuing education a reality, others chose to delay conscription eligibility through a draft-deferment policy for students first introduced during the Korean War (Davis and Dolbeare, 1968). Soon college enrollment numbers exceeded the growth of the traditional college-age population, with marked increases in male students. The college entry rate for men rose from 54 percent in 1963 to 62 percent in 1968.

Rapid increases in student population diversity and an anxious national climate soon challenged entrenched old-school philosophies. Social tensions and the war in Vietnam produced conflicting perceptions of civic responsibility and the concept of equal, individual rights. Students, sometimes radically, challenged academic leadership with demands for accountability and improvement. Under siege and under stress, institutional leaders were resistant and unwilling to abandon successful models of the past. J. B. Lon Hefferlin in his *Dynamics of Academic Reform* (1969) describes the purpose of colleges and universities as a "perpetuation of culture" steeped in custom and comfortable with precedent. By nature then, they remained resistant to the student requests for innovation and dealt with calls for change primarily when federal mandates made it unavoidable. As Hefferlin summarizes, "academic institutions are basically conservative in educational purpose and in support structures for innovation programs."

Still, by the early 1970s, innovations had clearly occurred, especially in areas of access and opportunity. Nationwide, entry requirements and prerequisites were lowered to assure admittance standards did not discriminate. Transcendence of the historic barriers of race, age, and socioeconomic factors was illustrated with an increasingly diverse student body. For any student fortunate enough to live near a tertiary institution or those willing and able to relocate, participation in higher education was now a reality. By the middle of the decade, the boards of directors at many higher education institutions wrestled to determine whether higher education should be viewed as a right, a privilege, or a duty. Some piloted college-outreach and certification-only programs, which brought brick-and-mortar extensions of the institutions to rural communities and inner-city neighborhoods.

The painful aftermath of the close of the Vietnam War and the specter of the Watergate scandal spread widespread distrust of hierarchical systems. Higher education was once again the subject of scrutiny. Academic quality and institutional responsibility moved to the public forefront. Practical, applicable skills were viewed as mandatory to further civic causes and ensure employability. No longer satisfied with mere assurances of access to higher education, students and politicians began to demand quantifiable elements to evaluate its effectiveness. The concept of academic success was radically changing from time spent in the classroom to tangible measures of the quality of the academic programming. While the groundswell for outcome-based education included primary and secondary schools, it was especially strong for higher education as scrutiny of costs of federal programming and consumer employment expectations were polarized by the softening economy.

By 1980, the country was in a recession and rapidly losing jobs. The inflation rate exceeded 13 percent, and the prime interest rate was greater than 15 percent. In his 1981 inaugural address, Ronald Reagan declared: "In this present crisis, government is not the solution to our problem; government is the problem." Higher education was facing a future of dwindling governmental support, escalated public scrutiny, and mounting calls for the cost justification of tuition and fees.

"THE IMPERATIVE FOR EDUCATION REFORM"

The election of Ronald Reagan brought federal scrutiny and public expectations for results-based higher education. There was a new federal mandate to reduce domestic spending on social programs, including educational support at all levels. Federal reductions in programming aid were deemed necessary to compensate for tax cuts designed to stimulate the economy. There was a growing movement to apply cost-effectiveness methodologies widely used in the business sector to all aspects of social programming. Higher education was increasingly viewed as an entrepreneurial business model. Consumers and taxpayers expected the effective delivery of practical tools to increase a participant's personal and professional success. Business leaders anticipated product-offering outcomes driven by end-user demand and state and federal agencies looked for ongoing, systemwide adherence to rigid cost-containment strategies.

It was the perfect storm. There was a clear governmental expectation of return on investment for the subsidization of higher education. The business sector questioned global higher-education rankings as increasing international competition–drained market share. Public pressure was mounting for assurances of academic effectiveness, especially in the area of job preparedness. Undergraduate enrollment, which had generally increased during the 1970s, fell from 10.8 million to 10.6 million between 1983 and 1985 (Snyder, Dillow, and Hoffman, 2009). Institutions scrambled to quantify their successes and tangibly illustrate both their value and their worth. Things were about to get worse. *A Nation at Risk: The Imperative for Education Reform*, the 1983 presidentially commissioned report of the National Commission on Excellence in Education, was scathing in its assessment of all aspects of education in America. Its assertions of multilevel failures in the educational system ushered in governmental scrutiny and common-man engagement with calls for reform (*Nation at Risk*, 1983).

The publication of *Integrity in the College Curriculum: A Report to the Academic Community* in 1985 by the Association of American Colleges (now the Association of American Colleges and Universities) presented a collegiate landscape that lacked quality, coherence, and accessibility and was validated by business leaders and recent graduates. It expressed the need for standardization and a "minimum required curriculum." Additionally, it advocated for the mandate of faculty-level accountability in all areas of student achievement. The report contributed additional momentum to the growing view that effectiveness of the higher education system had declined to a crisis-point situation. What resulted was increased public comfort with the standardized assessment of student-learning outcomes and the entrenchment of the assessment movement in higher education. This approach applied competency-based "success models" in use in vocational and trade schools since the 1970s to all institutions of higher learning. It was not easily reconciled with the long-accepted curricular models of liberal studies, a major and/

or minor specialization and electives to ensure a balance of academic diversity with disciplinary depth. Even more daunting was the need for rapid, diametric organizational rethinking at institutions where change was traditionally slow and unwieldy. At the highest organizational levels, an immediate shift in translating stakeholder concerns into practical institutional benefits was viewed as unpalatable and impossible.

To further complicate the situation, much of the burden of higher educational funding and oversight was shifting to individual states. Tuition costs continued to increase much faster than inflation. The public-duty concept of subsidizing accessible higher education was overridden by the reality of a declining state and local tax base. The duration of student attendance, overall costs of completion and the postgraduate employment rate became the new key metrics in governmental assessment of academic effectiveness. Graduation rates, freshman retention rates, and the percentage of students defaulting on their student loans became strong secondary indicators in determining institutional success and ensuring the availability of both state and federal funds. Many colleges and universities held the view that the federal requirements and employer endorsement of purely subjective success models greatly minimized the value of student individuality and dismissed institutional history and prestige. Still, immediate action was required. They faced an outcry for reform from government agencies, state boards, regional and professional accrediting bodies, and professional associations.

Classically, "reform" is a responsive process, planned and driven from the highest administrative levels and based on clear directives for change. Pronouncements to "own effectiveness" were passed down from administrators to teaching staff through mandated goal thresholds. With emphasis placed more heavily on the results and not the means, classroom methods and curricular coherence varied widely. Society called for reform, but what was needed was innovation. In many cases, leaders remained resistant and out of touch with the very processes they expected their staff to use. Technologies emerged that offered additional tools, new challenges, and potential instructional expansion. As pressure mounted on academic leadership to expedite the pace of institutional change, department heads and professors instinctually, and often without permission, began to forge progressive solutions.

The successful efforts of individual instructors often utilized strategies that bypassed institutional protocols. What resulted was a conflict between high-level academic control and the outcome-driven methods of grassroots innovators. The pace and pressure of change was contributing to a pervasive sense of chaos and frustration. A sanctioned structure was needed to ensure indigenous success could flourish and circulate. The solution lay in the integration of change-management and quality-improvement models flourishing in the business sector.

EAST MEETS WEST

Efforts to help rebuild Japanese business and infrastructure after World War II had allowed for the demonstrated effectiveness of a system of multilevel team input and flattened protocol levels. Developed by American statisticians W. Edwards Deming and Joseph M. Juran, Japan's "Kaizen" (improvement) Movement was a team-designed method of innovation and improvement. It advocated statistical process control, employee involvement, and a reduction in management protocols. After his successes in Japan, Deming brought his concept of continuous process improvement (CPI) to the United States, working with the Ford Motor Company. His system worked from the "bottom up" to increase the quality of an organization's outputs and eliminate activities that did not contribute value. Facing a shriveling economy and the mounting threat of international competition, many of the most successful companies had embraced CPI methodologies. By the early 1980s, it was widely replacing job-grading and process-valuation schemes utilized to increase industry efficiencies since the early 1950s. It provided processes to transcend institutional roadblocks and afforded front-line educators long awaited opportunities to tackle a litany of systemic, logistical, and resource barriers.

Educational teams could quickly and effectively restructure and redesign curricular initiatives to drive the gains required in measurable outcomes. Interdisciplinary and interdepartmental partnerships allowed fresh thinking through the utilization of collective experience, best-practice sharing, and negotiated approaches to modification and implementation of teaching methodologies. Increasingly, administrators recognized the logic that department heads, researchers, and professors had more investment and greater success in redesigning effective achievement strategies. Schools where these concepts were implemented began reaping the benefits of confirmable improvements and unexpected boosts in teacher morale. Outcomes improved in the classroom as increasing numbers of educators become confident in the speed and processes of innovation. Tertiary educators began to agree on universal teaching approaches that combined the targeting of learner preferences with employer-culture trait expectations. Common-practice philosophies were adopted, and the concepts of active and collaborative learning, cooperative education, and "learning communities" were widely accepted. As staff became engaged in making meaningful enhancements, feelings of panicked urgency gave way to motivated enthusiasm.

By the early 1990s, institutions were sanctioning faculty-development programming and introducing merit-based incentive plans. Staff training, empowerment, and recognition models were touted as employee benefits and used in recruitment and retention efforts. Higher education was evolving from a reluctant participant in the innovative process into a role model partner for business and industry. Trends in academic achievement once again began to satisfy popular expectations. Conscious and calculated applications of intellectual collaboration fashioned new markets for many institutions. The business sector began to recognize the cost benefits of outsourcing research, technologies, training, and curriculum development. Teachers employed similar tactics to increase levels of student engagement and permanently infuse them with institutional values and identity. Student numbers were on the rise with enrollment in degree-granting institutions increasing by 14 percent between 1987 and 1997 (Snyder, Dillow, and Hoffman, 2009).

Unfortunately, with increasing public endorsement and climbing enrollments, a profound understanding of the ongoing need for responsiveness remained incomplete. The crisis situation of higher education left powerful process-improvement tools in its wake. Meanwhile urgency waned with the decreasing momentum of academic reform. As innovation became dormant, these tools became dull. They would be called upon once again to meet increasing stakeholder expectations. The twenty-first century would systemically assault academia with technological advancements, economic crisis, war, and evolving student expectations. This time the need for a resharpening of the tools of reform is clearly felt at the highest levels. They are sounding the call to arms and scrambling to maximize efficiencies that will stimulate multilevel engagement and develop new thinking. Senior leaders in institutions and state systems see the challenges of innovation from a different perspective than faculty and staff. Leadership's job is not to invent a new way to teach a subject, structure a program, or provide a service but to create a climate, incentives, recognition, and commitment to new ways of doing things—a culture that encourages responsible risk taking and models out-of-the-box thinking.

As you continue on, this book leads you through discussion on the value of metrics and the impact of accreditation. It offers commentary and perspective from pace-setting administrators and highlights cutting-edge products, support services, and consortiums. Finally, it showcases innovative success stories "in the words" of those who converted collaborative concepts into demonstrated best practices.

PERSPECTIVES ON INNOVATION

Innovation and Popular Opinion
Stephan D. Spangehl and Allan M. Hoffman

"To change and to improve are two different things."

—German Proverb

The popular press treats *innovation* as one of those voguish terms, like *sustainability*, that is without negative connotations. Everyone overuses it—politicians, business people, educators, even workers—almost to the point where it is beginning to lose its meaning. Even one of the public icons of popular culture, Walt Disney's Epcot Center in Florida, includes a statue personifying innovation in its World Showcase's American Experience Pavilion. Much of the current buzz concerning innovation implies that it is the magic ingredient that made the United States outstanding and that, if we fail to continue to maintain world leadership in innovation, our future becomes bleak. However a brief look at the history of the concept indicates that the word was always employed in a set of broad senses, so it should come as no surprise that today it is used to describe a wide variety of activities.

Innovation is a key concept in economics, business, technology, and engineering, and in these discussions, the word *innovation* is often synonymous with the output of the process. However, simply coming up with new things—whether processes, tools, products, or systems—

is not enough, and economists and business people in particular stress the importance of implementation of a new idea rather than simply its creation. People who manage to establish the application of an innovation are often viewed as pioneers, sometimes even more than the original inventor.

Joseph Schumpeter is often credited with first defining *economic innovation* in *Theorie der Wirtschaftlichen Entwicklung* (*The Theory of Economic Development*, 1934) as a change in the thought process for doing something or the useful application of new inventions or discoveries. Schumpeter saw *innovation* covering:

1. the introduction of a new product or service with which consumers are not yet familiar, or of a new quality of an existing commodity;
2. the introduction of a new method of production, either one founded upon a new scientific discovery or simply a new way of handling commercial production of a commodity;
3. the opening of a new market where the particular approach to production had not previously been employed, even when this market has existed before;
4. the use of a new source of supply of raw materials or half-manufactured goods, regardless of whether this source already existed or was created by the innovation; and
5. the imposition of a new organization on any industry, for example the creation or destruction of monopoly positions.

Following Schumpeter, contributors to the scholarly literature on innovation typically distinguish between *invention* and *innovation*, using the latter to refer to ideas applied successfully in practice (vs. the simple development of a new idea). Consequently, something new must be substantially different to be called *innovative* in many fields. In economics the change must increase value for either customers or producers. In virtually all uses, *innovation* implies *positive* change, making someone or something better, and thus all changes are not automatically innovation—even though there is a widespread temptation for those benefiting from any change to hype them as such. The connection of many innovations to increased productivity makes much current economic thinking view innovation as the fundamental source of increasing economic wealth, both for individuals and for entire societies. Much of the current worry about U.S. higher education boils down to a belief that U.S. economic and political strength in the world will stagnate and decline if Asian educational systems outproduce the United States in the STEM disciplines—science, technology, engineering, and mathematics—which many see as the drivers of innovation.

INNOVATION IN THE EYES OF THE SPELLINGS COMMISSION

Those focusing on higher education typically comment on how other enterprises—particularly manufacturing and health care—have experienced growth and better performance through improvements in efficiency, productivity, outsourcing, competitive positioning, market share, and quality. The nineteen-member Commission on the Future of Higher Education appointed by U.S. Secretary of Education Margaret Spellings was "charged with developing a comprehensive national strategy for postsecondary education that will meet the needs of America's diverse population and also address the economic and workforce needs of the country's future." Its final report in 2006, which concluded that "for the country as a whole, future economic growth depends on our ability to sustain excellence, innovation, and leadership in higher education," was filled with recommendations extremely critical of the importance U.S. higher education has placed on innovation. In all, the report uses *innovation*, *innovate*, or *innovative* over fifty times.

Here is a sampling:

- "As higher education evolves in unexpected ways, this new landscape demands innovation and flexibility from the institutions that serve the nation's learners" (Spellings, 2006, p. xi).
- "Policymakers and higher education leaders should develop, at the institutional level, new and innovative means to control costs, improve productivity, and increase the supply of higher education" (Spellings, 2006, p. 20).
- "The commission recommends that FIPSE prioritize, disseminate, and promote best practices in innovative teaching and

learning models as well as the application of high-quality learn-
ing-related research in such rapidly growing areas as neurosci-
ence, cognitive science and organizational sciences" (Spellings,
2006, p. 25).

- "Institutions should harness the power of information technology by sharing educational resources among institutions, and use
distance learning to meet the educational needs of rural students
and adult learners, and to enhance workforce development. Effective use of information technology can improve student learning,
reduce instructional costs, and meet crucial workforce needs. We
urge states and institutions to establish course redesign programs
using technology based, learner-centered principles drawing upon
the innovative work already being done by organizations such as
the National Center for Academic Transformation. Additionally,
we urge institutions to explore emerging interdisciplinary fields
such as services sciences, management and engineering and to
implement new models of curriculum development and delivery"
(Spellings, 2006, pp. 25–26).

- "We call on the business community to become directly and fully
engaged with government and higher education leaders in developing innovative structures for delivering 21st century educational
services—and in providing the necessary financial and human resources for that purpose" (Spellings, 2006, p. 29).

The Spellings Report's "Findings Regarding Innovation" (Spellings,
2006, pp. 15–16) are so unqualifiedly damning that they deserve to be
studied carefully in full (see textbox 2.1).

Technology—the use of computers in general and distance education
in particular—appears to be the only redeeming innovation the commission can discover in higher education: There is no mention of assessment, learning styles, writing across the curriculum, student–faculty
research, or many other changes in academia over the past decades, perhaps because these did not translate immediately into the cost efficiencies and increased productivity (i.e., more graduates) that appears to
narrow the commission's perceptions of what constitutes an innovation.
Given the presence of Nicholas Donofrio, executive vice president of
innovation and technology at the IBM Corporation, on the commission

TEXTBOX 2.1. THE SPELLINGS REPORT'S "FINDINGS REGARDING INNOVATION"

American higher education has taken little advantage of important innovations that would increase institutional capacity, effectiveness, and productivity. Government and institutional policies created during a different era are impeding the expansion of models designed to meet the nation's workforce needs. In addition, policymakers and educators need to do more to build America's capacity to compete and innovate by investing in critical skill sets and basic research.

- Institutions as well as government agencies have failed to sustain and nurture innovation in our colleges and universities. The commission finds that the results of scholarly research on teaching and learning are rarely translated into practice, especially for those working at the grassroots level in fields such as teacher preparation and math and science education. We also find that little of the significant research of the past decade in areas such as cognitive science, neurosciences, and organizational theory is making it into American classroom practice, whether at the K–12 level or in colleges and universities.
- The commission finds that with the exception of several promising practices, many of our postsecondary institutions have not embraced opportunities for innovation, from new methods of teaching and content delivery to technological advances to meeting the increasing demand for lifelong learning. We also find that for their part, both state and federal policymakers have failed to make supporting innovation a priority by adequately providing incentives for individuals, employers, and institutions to pursue more opportunities for innovative, effective, and efficient practice.
- Traditional academic calendars and schedules often result in inefficient use of an institution's physical plant and learning programs that are less than optimal.
- Barriers to the recognition of transfer credits between different types of institutions pose challenges to students and prevent

institutions from increasing capacity. Students too often receive conflicting information about credit-transfer policies between institutions, leading to an unknown amount of lost time and money (and additional federal financial aid) in needlessly repeated course work. Underlying the information confusion are institutional policies and practice on student transfers that are too often inconsistently applied, even within the same institution.

- Accreditation and federal and state regulations, while designed to assure quality in higher education, can sometimes impede innovation and limit the outside capital investment that is vital for expansion and capacity building.
- Fewer American students are earning degrees in the STEM fields (science, technology, engineering, mathematics), medicine, and other disciplines critical to global competitiveness, national security, and economic prosperity. Even as the Bureau of Labor Statistics projects that 16 of the 30 fastest-growing jobs in the next decade will be in the health professions, current and projected shortages of physicians, registered nurses and other medical specialists may affect the quality of care for the increasingly aging population of baby boomers.
- It is fundamental to U.S. economic interests to provide world-class education while simultaneously providing an efficient immigration system that welcomes highly educated individuals to our nation. Foreign-born students represent about half of all graduate students in computer sciences, and over half of the doctorate degrees awarded in engineering. Almost 30 percent of the actively employed science and engineering doctorate holders in the U.S. are foreign born. However, current limits on employer-sponsored visas preclude many U.S. businesses from hiring many of these graduates, which may discourage some talented students from attending our universities.
- At a time when innovation occurs increasingly at the intersection of multiple disciplines (including business and social sciences), curricula and research funding remain largely contained in individual departments.

and the absence of leaders in new directions in higher education, the report's boosterism in this area should not be surprising.

The report's final recommendations on innovation (Spellings, 2006, pp. 21–27) sound as if the majority was convinced not merely that higher education had failed to rise to the level of creativity needed but that external regulation—from state and federal government and from accreditors—was at fault. Nowhere does the commission acknowledge that an 800+-year-old conservative tradition in higher education may play a role in the industry's failure to jump on the bandwagon for the "latest new thing." The report's summary highlights the Spellings Commission's most critical concerns regarding innovation:

- "Finally, we found that numerous barriers to investment in innovation risk hampering the ability of postsecondary institutions to address national workforce needs and compete in the global marketplace. Too many of our colleges and universities have not embraced opportunities to be entrepreneurial, from testing new methods of teaching and content delivery to meeting the increased demand for lifelong learning. For their part, state and federal policymakers have also failed to make supporting innovation a priority" (Spellings, 2006, pp. 4–5).
- "Accreditation, along with federal and state regulation, can impede creative new approaches as well" (Spellings, 2006, p. 5).
- "In our view, correcting shortcomings in educational quality and promoting innovation requires a series of related steps, beginning with some of the accountability mechanisms that are summarized below and discussed at greater length later in this report. In addition, we urge postsecondary institutions to make a commitment to embrace new pedagogies, curricula, and technologies to improve student learning" (Spellings, 2006, p. 4).
- "We recommend that America's colleges and universities embrace a culture of continuous innovation and quality improvement. We urge these institutions to develop new pedagogies, curricula and technologies to improve learning, particularly in the areas of science and mathematics. At the same time, we recommend the development of a national strategy for lifelong learning designed to

keep our citizens and our nation at the forefront of the knowledge revolution" (Spellings, 2006, p. 5).

The reaction to the Spellings Report from the academic community was hostile, and its highest-ranking member from academe, American Council on Education's then-president David Ward, was the only one of the commission's nineteen members to refuse to sign it. Discussion in the higher education was dismissing, not merely of its criticisms of the failure of higher education to innovate, but of criticisms of accountability, transparency, lack of information on which the public could base its educational decisions, low learning goals and expectations, financial stewardship, accreditation, and other criticisms it leveled. There were some attempts to respond, mild and not terribly innovative ones at best, such as the Voluntary System of Accountability (VSA) put forth by the American Association of State College and Universities (AASCU), which put into concise Web reports information mostly already available on the U.S. Department of Education website.

In negotiated rule-making concerning accreditation that Spellings scheduled before Congress had acted on a new 2008 Higher Education Opportunity Act (HEOA), she pushed, for changes that would implement some of the commission's recommendations. The DuPont Circle higher education agencies found Senate support (led by Lamar Alexander of Tennessee, in a June 14, 2007, letter to Margaret Spellings) to get the secretary to drop her plans. Ultimately, the new HEOA passed in August 2008 contained language guaranteeing specifically that institutions must set their own learning expectations for students and that future National Advisory Committees on Institutional Quality and Integrity (NACIQI, the group that advises the secretary of education on recognizing accreditation agencies) would have a third of its members appointed by the House and a third by the Senate, reducing the influence the Department of Education had in previously appointing all NACIQI members. Much of the academic community breathed a sigh of relief, and the common wisdom was that higher education "had ducked the bullet" that the administration was ready to fire at it.

Unfortunately, in all the politicking that surrounded the Spellings Commission and its aftermath, an honest assessment of the role, strength, and potential for higher education innovation was lost. Read-ers of the commission's report are easily left with the impression that higher education is a moribund industry when compared with other innovative enterprises (except, perhaps, "with the exception of several promising practices" that the commission report fails to list).

It does higher education no real service to silence the issues that the Spellings Commission raised; they are all still problems, perhaps worse now in a worsened economy. There is every sign that current and future U.S. leaders, regardless of political party or philosophy, cannot continue to ignore the problems in higher education, although the current voracious attack on for-profit institutions may serve, for a while, to distract everyone's attention from the more fundamental problems shared by all higher education.

The pressure for higher education to approach its challenges in fresh ways continues to increase. As frustration on both sides mounts, policymakers' desire for policies that can serve as "magic bullets" intensifies. The Spellings Commission's repeated invocation of innovation in its report has some of this flavor: Remove the "barriers" to innovation (including quality assurance regulation and the academy's traditional self-invented standards), and innovation will flourish and everything will be fine. As Diane Ravitch so well explains in *The Death and Life of the Great American School System: How Testing and Choice Are Undermining Education* (2010), policymakers, unwilling to recognize that improving education requires thousands of incremental changes and endless hard work, look constantly for global solutions—uniform testing of students, merit pay for teachers, competition from "charter schools," and so on—as the macrolevel innovation that miraculously drives all the innovations needed to make performance changes at operational levels.

One useful consequence of Spellings should be recognition that a great many innovations have already been implemented in today's higher education institutions, and more are created and applied daily. Some, perhaps the vast majority, of these innovations are small: better ways to do things that academia always recognized as worth doing, minor ways to reduce the cost or improve the efficiency of existing activities and processes, and new ways to do things that make sense and add value but are rarely earth-shaking. Like evolution, the road to a vastly improved higher education system that meets the needs of the twenty-first century and those that follow it won't come about through a single innovation but rather through a constellation of small ones. What's necessary is more awareness of all the small improvements that have already been created, implemented, and tested, often with no one but those directly involved noticing. This book is a beginning in giving all of this innovation the attention it deserves and hopefully restoring the role of innovation in higher education to the pedestal it has earned and deserves. U.S. higher education still has much room to improve, but it is hardly the anti-innovation, backward-looking industry that some in the government and press have characterized. People who devote their lives to the creation, transmission, and preservation of knowledge tend to be first among those who seek new answers to old problems, and those are the people upon whom operation of U.S. colleges and universities depend.

3

DOES ACCREDITATION INHIBIT INNOVATION?

Stephen D. Spangehl and Henry J. Lindborg

"No snowflake in an avalanche ever feels responsible."

—George Burns

A*ccredited* is a descriptor of colleges and universities that most people understand only vaguely, somewhat the way they understand *USDA Inspected* or *Underwriters' Laboratory Approved.* The public appreciates that these are desirable stamps, but few people grasp what they actually represent—what criteria must be met to warrant them, how disinterested and unbiased are those making the judgments, what training and oversight do the judges receive, or what happens when they are judged as failing to meet prescribed expectations. Even fewer recognize the consequences, privileges, and responsibilities of a higher education institution's being accredited or what that status might mean to them personally—in hiring a college graduate, in paying for an employee education benefit program, in selecting an institution to attend, or in helping family and friends make similar life-changing but largely irreversible decisions about college.

Traditionally, the public judges higher education by reputation, what David Garvin classified as "perceived quality." Because institutions are diverse and we lack widely agreed-upon and easily articulated performance standards, many people base their evaluations on a combination of indirect measures, ranging from name recognition, campus social life, the ranking of sports teams, and high admission standards to the number of alumni in the "power elite" or the starting salaries of graduates. At the same time, many assume that the accreditation stamp is a mark of *quality assurance*, indicating that an institution conforms to a single set of rigorous standards—however poorly these may be understood. A review of the history and types of higher education accreditation reveals a more complex picture, however.

Accreditation in the United States is the result of a set of historical events, some accidental, some purposeful. At present, there are three kinds of accreditation agencies—regional, national, and specialized—all operating independently of each other, often on the same institutions.

Regional accreditation is the oldest, with three of the six regional accrediting commissions founded in 1895. As their name implies, each commission provides accreditation to entire institutions that have home bases within their regions or groups of states. The largest (the Higher Learning Commission, formerly the North Central Association) accredits over one thousand institutions in nineteen states, while the smallest, the Western Association of Schools and Colleges, accredits institutions only in California and Hawaii (and a scattering of U.S. Pacific Ocean territories like Guam). There is a commission for New England, one for the "old south," one for the northwest and western states (including Alaska), and one for the Middle Atlantic States stretching from New York to Maryland and D.C. Inexplicably, the smallest has two separate commissions, one for two-year colleges and the other for baccalaureate and higher institutions, while each of the larger regions have only one commission each, accrediting all types of institutions. All the commissions are private, not-for-profit membership corporations, and the institutions they accredit select their boards, provide their funding, determine their processes and standards, and provide the "peer reviewers" that judge whether the institutions meet the standards and deserve to be accredited. Accreditation by a regional commission covers all of an institution's programs and all of its campuses and operations (including distance education programs)—across the United States or around the world. Regional accreditation is an all-or-nothing business, with no shade of gray or rankings: Either an institution is accredited, or it is not.

Regional is a somewhat misleading term for these commissions: Although the six regions are separately governed, autonomous, and sometimes fiercely independent, all use similar processes and standards. Their standards are minimums, threshold requirements for institutions to operate, qualitative more than quantitative, and more specific about resource requirements than institutional performance. The standards guide peer reviewers in determining subjectively what is *appropriate*, *reasonable*, or *typical* in light of the institution's declared mission or purposes, letting institutional public/private, secular/religious, proprietary/nonprofit, large/small, and urban/rural differences rationalize uneven judgments. Maximizing quality is not the primary concern, although the regionals all let their reviewers provide advice on improvement along with their judgments. The level of *quality assurance* that regional accreditation provides is unclear, although most would admit that accredited institutions are less risky than those who never sought accreditation—or lost it. However, no one would suggest that all accredited institutions have equal quality or that the thresholds used to judge them are particularly rigorous.

In addition, fifty or more specialized (or program) accreditors set standards for specific programs within larger institutions (or in institutions so specialized that they offer only one kind of program, such as independent law schools not connected with universities). Many of the specialized accrediting agencies are outgrowths of organizations dedicated to the welfare and support of professional groups like lawyers, dentists, physicians, social workers, and teachers. Although every specialized agency claims to be supporting high standards in its profession, critics accuse them of setting standards to first protect their professions. For professions where licensure is required to practice (law, medicine, nursing, teaching, chiropractic, pharmacy), the specialized agencies have often worked hard to ensure that only graduates of the programs they accredit can be licensed; in turn, their rigorous resource requirements for programs may have the effect of limiting access to their profession. For example, enrollment limitations on medical schools have forced U.S. students seeking to be physicians to go abroad and then jump licensing hurdles when they return to the United States to practice. A few specialized agencies accredit programs in fields without licensure (such as business studies in management, marketing, finance—everything except accounting), and so accreditation in some cases may denote prestige rather than enable employment. The specialized agencies all accredit nationwide, and some have even extended their operations to programs in non-U.S. institutions.

National accreditation is a more recent invention, created to accredit the institutions that the regionals would not—originally for-profit institutions and postsecondary schools not offering associate or higher degrees. Now all of the regionals have accredited proprietary (for-profit) institutions, so the distinction between regionals and nationals has blurred.

In particular, the emergence of for-profit degree-granting institutions—and the capital venture firms that acquire and direct them—has created major tension in the traditional picture. Accreditation developed when the higher education community was relatively homogeneous, when conceptions of what was required to create, staff, and operate an institution was "common sense" to professors and higher education administrators. Sending peer teams with vague standards to review each other worked because the range of practice and the community of practitioners were both narrow. But the emergence of national proprietary chains, creating accelerated courses and programs and staffing them in ways radically different from traditional practice, has created serious strains.

New models call into question the need for full-time faculty, full-time well-prepared students, general education courses, extracurricular activities and services, face-to-face student–teacher contact, and many of the other characteristics that have been hallmarks of U.S. higher education. Accreditation has been hard pressed to keep pace. More crucially, advanced postsecondary education has become increasingly recognized as a basic need for all citizens, so much so that both presidential candidates in the 2008 race called higher education a "human right." The ability of the United States to compete internationally, in an environment where only "knowledge workers" earn wages higher than what is considered subsistence levels and employment can be electronically outsourced anywhere in the world, has made policymakers acutely aware of their responsibility to see that citizens not merely have *access* to higher education but actually receive it—and the credentials that testify to it.

Since World War II, the federal government has provided funds—first to GIs, now to everyone—to encourage and support obtaining a higher education. To be sure the funds were not squandered, they come with rules: They must be spent in institutions where the quality of education meets reasonable standards. To avoid getting the government into the business of setting educational standards, since World War II it has used the existing accrediting agencies to perform this "gatekeeping" task. The Higher Education Opportunities Act (HEOA), the national legislation that provides over $80 billion in federal funds for higher education grants and loans, established a National Advisory Committee on Institutional Quality and Integrity (NACIQI), whose role is to review and recognize accrediting agencies that seek to be "gatekeepers" for federal funds. The agencies must be "federally recognized" every five years in order for the students who enroll in the institutions or programs they accredit to receive federal grants or federally guaranteed loans. Thus accreditation by a federal-recognized agency is not simply a matter of prestige but an essential requirement for institutions seeking to attract any but the richest students. All regional and national accreditors seek federal recognition, as do some specialized agencies whose programs are offered in specialized or otherwise unaccredited organizations.

Unlike most modern industrialized countries, the United States is hampered in establishing national goals for advanced education of its citizens. The constitution, framed around circumstances in 1789, made oversight of education a state responsibility and excluded it from federal control. So where China, Norway, or South Africa can establish educational targets for their citizens—and enact the mechanisms to achieve their targets—Congress and the executive branch are limited to providing funds that encourage states and private organizations to "do the right things" to make citizens educationally competitive in the twenty-first century. Thus the federal reconditioning of accrediting agencies as gatekeepers for federal funds becomes one of the few means through which the national government can influence higher education policy, practice, and performance.

Making accreditation into something more than compliance with threshold standards has always been a goal the agencies hold dear, but the difficulties in achieving it have been great. When confronted with a series of activities that, if things go badly, could effectively put an institution out of business, most colleges and universities are unwilling to take risks. Accreditors tell institutions that self-study and site visits are tools for improvement, the means to identify what is not working well so that it can be fixed. But faced with the prospect of a team of strangers coming to campus and, after two or three days of review, rendering an accreditation recommendation with crucial consequences generally tempers the enthusiasm of institutions to be searchingly self-critical.

Some agencies, however, seek new ways to marry minimalist quality assurance with quality performance and productivity improvement. The Higher Learning Commission's alternative accreditation maintenance process, its Academic Quality Improvement Program, isolates compliance activities in order to allow institutions to work on innovation and improvement in an atmosphere free from immediate risks to their continued accreditation, blending traditional accreditation with the philosophy and techniques of the Baldrige Program. (The Baldrige Performance Excellence Program, formerly the Malcolm Baldrige National Quality Award, is the program operated by the National Institute of Standards and Technology in the U.S. Department of Commerce to teach businesses how to apply the principles of quality management to improve performance results. Since 2001, it has given Baldrige Awards to model primary, secondary, and higher education institutions as well as business and health-care organizations.) The Southern Association of Colleges and Schools has introduced institutionally designed quality enhancement projects as a requirement for continued accreditation, and the Western Association of Schools and Colleges' Accrediting Commission for Senior Colleges and Universities has reengineered its processes so that it conducts separate site visits for compliance and improvement.

Many of the specialized agencies—most notably the Accreditation Board for Engineering and Technology and the Teacher Education Accreditation Council—have built standards and processes designed to stimulate continuous improvement, and many of the health science accrediting agencies show indications of similar future directions. Yet the overall higher education industry, both individual colleges and universities and the agencies that accredit them, show high levels of self-satisfaction with their past behaviors and their accomplishment of having made twentieth-century U.S. higher education the envy of the world. It is unclear whether continuation of past U.S. practices enables this important industry to compete internationally with vigorous new developments in European and Asian higher education.

Moreover, it is doubtful that past levels of productivity and student achievement—the proportion of American students our institutions graduate and the levels of those graduates' knowledge and skills—can continue to keep the United States competitive with countries rapidly reengineering their higher education systems to achieve previously unimaginable quality and productivity levels. How U.S. accreditation as currently organized and practiced can address these and the other twenty-first–century educational challenges remains a mystery. Moreover, it becomes increasingly difficult to see how accreditation can continue to promote, or at least allow, innovation while it continues to satisfy the U.S. Department of Education's increasingly restrictive requirements for what it seeks in a "gatekeeper" for overly stretched financial aid funding.

4

MEASURING SUCCESS

Stephen D. Spangehl

"Success is on the far side of failure."

—Thomas Watson Sr.

THE VALUE OF METRICS

One of the prerequisites for an innovation climate is an unwillingness to settle for the status quo, to "let well enough alone." Metrics can help create the sense of urgency that inspires employees to come up with new ideas, new approaches, and new methods. Metrics can let people know how well their organization currently performs—not simply what percentage of the students graduate or what percentage go on to jobs and careers in their field of study, but also an awareness of far more de-tailed performance metrics that might be directly influenced by changes in policies or how the faculty and staff behave. Knowing that 60 percent of all students graduate is helpful, but understanding that the 60 percent rate averages together a 95 percent rate for white females under thirty, a 20 percent rate for black males under thirty, and a 45 percent rate for males of all colors between thirty and forty-five begins to shed light on where the institution might direct action that would result in a higher overall graduation rate. Gross performance statistics alone don't provide actionable targets for improvement.

But simply *knowing* an institution's own performance does not necessarily create the urgency that inspires innovation. Institutions can become complacent, knowing they equal or slightly exceed their own past performance, even in a time when they are falling far behind the performance of the institutions with which they compete. Comparative data—what higher education likes to call *benchmarks*—can tell an institution whether its current performance is head and shoulders above that of others or at ground level, far below what others are achieving and what the institution itself should be satisfied with. An institution graduating 60 percent of its freshman females entering from high school can be proud if comparable institutions are graduating 40 percent of this cohort, but it should be ashamed if others are achieving an 80- or 90-percent rate. Knowing the existence of performance gaps that are closable—because more successful institutions' activities and processes might easily be duplicated or improved upon—is a powerful stimulus for innovation.

Innovation can take the form of adopting best practices already in use by others or coming up with brand-new, previously untried mechanisms that allow performance levels to increase. A variety of innovations owe their genesis to situations in which institutions were dissatisfied with current performance and experimented to find ways to improve. Some effective examples include the following:

- Northwest Missouri State University developed programming requiring high-risk students to take group tutorial sections tied to the general education courses they were taking.
- The University of South Carolina's First Year Experience Program uncovered and focused attention on opportunities to build stronger involvement on the part of entering freshmen.
- There are numerous innovations in the structure and delivery of remedial-developmental education, many discovered and catalogued by the National Center for Developmental Education at Appalachian State University in Boone, North Carolina.

There are a host of freshman orientation courses designed to ease the high school–college transition and others that target the tendency of new students to assimilate to behaviors unlikely to improve their academic success. Metrics dramatically can show people when they shouldn't be satisfied with current performance or what levels of performance actually are possible. They override faculty and staff contentions that the "way things were and the way they are now is how they will remain forever." Metrics offer tangible tracking when addressing institutional improvements and the opportunity for incentives to dream up new approaches.

BENCHMARKS AND BENCHMARKING

Benchmarking can be one of the greatest potential spurs to institutional innovation. Knowing that others have found solutions that let them excel in performance can give an institution both the motivation to improve as well as the knowledge that breakthrough improvement *is* possible. Some forms of benchmarking can actually stimulate the innovative ideas themselves, while others simply can provide an institution with data that suggests improvement is possible. In contemporary higher education, *benchmarking* is a much-used label for at least *three* very different crucial concepts. Just knowing whether a college or university is benchmarking isn't instructive unless we know what *kind* of benchmarking the institution is doing, why they are benchmarking, and what the consequences may be. When peers share their counsel for continuing improvement, any institutional uncertainty in interpreting what *benchmarking* means could make their advice confusing and perhaps even ineffectual.

A Little History

Although it sounds like it should have originated among carpenters, the word *benchmark* first appeared in written English in 1864, designating the mark that was cut in a rock wall or post and from which land surveyors took all of their subsequent measurements. Outside of higher education, the term today refers most commonly to the product comparisons that computer and software designers calculate to explain why theirs (machine, program, card, peripheral) is faster, more powerful, and a better buy. In all current uses of *benchmark* and *benchmarking*, *measuring* and *comparing* are important elements.

Benchmarking with Comparable Institutions

In this first of three concepts, *benchmark* refers to one or more institutions that people compare with their own college or university. Because comparisons can be on a variety of dimensions and levels, an institution could identify benchmarks to compare its own tuition rates, its faculty–student ratio, its alumni giving, or any other measurable variable. Often, however, institutions try to identify all-purpose benchmarks, peer institutions that can serve as the basis for a spectrum of comparisons.

Many public institutions have a set of benchmarks identified for them by their state coordinating or advisory board, a group usually designated for the purpose of the comparison, like salary benchmarks or budget benchmarks. In choosing these benchmarks, the state's goal is often to limit the institution's appetite by establishing parameters on the size of requests. In turn, the institution lobbies for its own set of target benchmark institutions, models for the kind of institution it would like to be like. These benchmarks and benchmark institutions are usually better funded and more prestigious than the benchmarker choosing them; their purpose is to give an institution something concrete to shoot for, a vision of the kind of institution they could become. In addition, these benchmarked institutions are typically funded at higher levels, so the benchmarking institution can make the case for "catch up" monies.

However they are chosen, identifying benchmark institutions should be done with caution because the process oversimplifies the complex ways in which two institutions can differ. Selecting peers for all comparison purposes is difficult, and much confusion results from such efforts; comparison can mislead badly unless the purpose of the comparison is focused (e.g., identify similarly endowed institutions in order to gauge whether their return-on-investment from endowments is better or worse than those with similar sums to invest). Furthermore, a focused comparison may still not be logical even though institutions may be similar in some aspects. Benchmarking institutions that have similar enrollments in order to set target salary levels for faculty makes little sense; enrollment has little to do either with an institution's resources for faculty salaries or for the work faculty must do, which is affected by workload policies and faculty–student ratios (dependent, in turn, on the total number of faculty). Trying to find institutions where all of the variables match [same enrollment, same ratios, same budget, same locale, and same institutional control (public, private, nonprofit, or for-profit)] tends to shrink the pool of potential comparisons to zero.

Benchmarking with Comparative Data

There are sets of questions concerning performance that come up continually in every higher education institution: Where are we in relation to our goals? Are we doing well? Are we improving? Are we making progress quickly enough? Are we succeeding or failing in our task? Are we growing, learning, and developing? These are the questions students ask about themselves, the questions that faculty ask about their students and courses, and (more and more, we hope, as a result of the North Central Association of Colleges and Schools' assessment initiative) the questions that institutions ask about their academic and support programs. Using benchmarking with comparative data to answer general questions like these depends on (1) knowing in which direction the goal lies, (2) having a realistic sense of how far away that goal is, and (3) assessing how quickly the institution is approaching it. If reducing debt or raising enrollment or providing more effective developmental assistance to underprepared students or designing educationally effective new degree programs is the goal, then it is imperative for a serious institution to measure whether it is moving toward the goals.

Doing so requires, first, a set of metrics—measures that enable the institution to chart the progress it makes. Metrics are measures and come in a variety of versions; it is up to each institution to find ways to measure the things it believes are real indicators of its progress accurately enough to make the measurement useful. Some metrics are counts—dollars in reserve or square feet of classroom space or students enrolled—while some can be ratios or other measures computed from a set of more simple measures, as complex as degree program cost per instructional credit hour or a combined measure of faculty salaries, teaching loads, class sizes, incidental instructional costs, classroom space used, and so on for each academic program. Measures like these allow internal comparisons (Is our biology program more profitable than philosophy? Have the changes we made in student recruiting produced more students than the old approach?), and they ground planning and decision making in facts rather than in hopes, fears, and vague impressions. More slippery metrics, such as those based on people's perceptions and opinions (students' and anyone else's satisfaction with teachers, curriculum, food service, parking, campus events, facilities) can, if questions and scales are thought out carefully and data are gathered fairly, produce rich and useful information that may target which areas need improvement or identify which alternatives hold most promise.

Alone, measurement is not enough to chart movement. To perceive progress or slippage, there must exist something to which the institution can compare today's measurement. As the saying goes, "You can't tell which way the train is going just by looking at the tracks." The comparisons can be internal ("more graduates in computer science than in political science") or with the institution's own past record ("fewer students using the library than in any previous year") or external ("more technical design graduates found related employment within six months than in 60 percent of other institutions offering tech design programs"). External comparisons can be local, regional, national, or "world class." Like other benchmarks, selecting comparisons for metrics depends on an institution's purposes, and its purposes can often be inferred from its choices. The complacent college that wants to puff about its accomplishments (whether they are significant or trivial) will choose comparative data from benchmarks that make it look good, that show it far ahead of its pack. The institution focused on maximizing its effectiveness will seek out comparison data from the leaders in whatever area it is analyzing—trying to stretch itself by getting numerical goals from those who are best at recruiting or fundraising or teaching students to write or cutting attrition—and setting targets that show what is possible rather than what has already been achieved.

Many institutions will use both, of course: for marketing, the easy comparisons that make it look good; for planning and evaluation, the tough ones that challenge it. The comparative data a serious institution uses in its self-study process, the comparisons it shares with a team of peers with whom it is trying to establish its seriousness as an institution focused on improvement, ought to be the comparisons that make it stretch. In Robert Browning's (1855) "Andrea del Sarto," his admonition that a "man's reach must exceed his grasp, or what's a heaven for?" is equally true for colleges and universities.

Knowing how much an institution underperforms others on any particular measure is useful because it focuses on an area in which the institution can improve. Knowing that retention of freshmen into their second year is only 25 percent may signal a problem, but knowing that similar institutions are retaining 80 percent makes it a dire situation, though it is only a minor challenge if peers are retaining 30 percent.

Benchmarking for Best Practices

The third contemporary use of the word *benchmark* refers to a "continuous, systematic process for evaluating the products, services, and work processes of organizations that are recognized as representing exemplary methods and systems for the purpose of organizational improvement" (Spendolini, 1992, p. 9). For example, if a college wishes to improve the way it recruits, interviews, and selects its faculty, it might launch a project to discover the best practices used by organizations recognized as national or world leaders for their personnel processes—with the intention of copying or adapting their recipe for success in its own operations.

Neither simple nor quick, benchmarking best practices normally requires at least five steps.

1. Select a Target Process.   Determining which process to benchmark is the usual beginning. It could be new program development, teacher evaluation, placement of underprepared students, student recordkeeping, purchasing, maintenance of grounds, searching for new faculty, or any of the other hundreds of discrete processes that make an institution function. To do this step well, an institution needs to see itself through "process" lenses, then identify a process or system crucial to its success—ideally one in need of improvement and (perhaps most important) a process whose "owners" are willing to change if benchmarking can uncover better ways to accomplish the process's objectives.

2. Form a Benchmarking Team.   Next, the institution must form a benchmarking team, ideally one that includes the "process owners" who will have to adapt and apply whatever is learned from benchmarking. If these process owners are not an active part of the discovery process, it becomes unlikely that whatever is learned will be applied, nor does experience indicate that it is enough for senior leaders to say "we have now discovered new secrets our underlings should embrace to be more productive." Because benchmarking best practices is a costly and complex business, it is becoming increasingly common for groups of organizations with shared goals to form cooperative benchmarking teams or to engage in cooperative projects, often with assistance from a benchmarking consulting firm. For example, the financial aid departments of a number of colleges may work together to identify best practices, focusing on a different aid process each year. Group projects work best where competition is not an issue; understandably, colleges competing for the same recruits are unlikely to pool their best ideas for recruiting.

3. Select Organizations to Study. Next, the team must identify benchmarking partners—organizations that are world, national, or regional leaders in using the particular process being benchmarked. Often this is the most difficult—and creative—piece of the benchmarking work. Research studies, published performance data, surveys, awards, publicity, and even word of mouth are sources of information that can help identify the leaders in using a particular process. In the world of commerce, industry observers, suppliers, dealers, and customers can often point the way to a leader, as can market research and watchdog groups, standard-setting organizations, the press, unions, state and federal government agencies, the financial community, and industry promotional and regulatory agencies. Identifying leaders for the processes crucial to higher education requires diligent research. Luckily, it is often exactly the kind of research in which faculty are (or can quickly become) expert.

Thinking outside the box of our personal histories, our work experiences, and what we've learned is successful is crucial for this step. Often, the organizations currently using the best practices for a process in which a college is interested will not turn out to be another college. Therefore thinking about the business areas in which process leaders might be found requires a benchmarking team to abandon its stereotypes and look beyond striking (but superficial) differences in organizations. One group of colleges seeking to benchmark student services decided to include the hotel industry because the processes for identifying guests' needs and meeting them seemed a promising area for new insights. Ultimately they identified Ritz-Carlton as the leader in the field and learned much from the processes this successful firm uses to provide customized guest services. Similarly, when Xerox benchmarked order fulfillment and warehousing operations, it selected L. L. Bean as a leader to study in spite of the apparent disconnect between outdoor clothes and office equipment.

This identification of work processes of noncompetitors is sometimes referred to as *functional* (or *generic*) benchmarking because it concentrates on a functional area, such as marketing, manufacturing, human resources, or design/engineering. Its objective is to identify best practices in *any* type of organization that has established a reputation for excellence in the areas being benchmarked. Many benchmarking consultants insist on including one or more "out-of-industry" partners, and following their counsel has often led benchmarking studies to their most dramatic breakthrough improvements. This should not be surprising: A great new technique used by a college for, say, placing new students in the appropriate courses is likely to be known of and copied by other colleges. It is far less likely that colleges will learn of a breakthrough diagnostic process being developed and used successfully in the hospital business or in automotive repair or some other noneducational enterprise. Institutions that promote faculty and staff creativity, cross-fertilization, and interdisciplinary thinking will particularly enjoy this aspect of benchmarking.

4. Document, Analyze, and Understand the Partners' Practices. What follows next is the heart of the "best practice" work: making contact with the partners; gaining their confidence; and getting them to allow the collection of "best practice" information, techniques, and secrets. Normally, this part of the benchmarking work is done first via surveys and questionnaires, then by one or more carefully planned and efficiently conducted visits to the benchmark partners. Once the successful techniques and "secrets" have been catalogued, it then requires serious analysis to identify what practices underpin the partner's success and what else in the partner organization's culture must be emulated to "borrow" these secrets.

5. Bring the Learning Home. Finally, benchmarking must lead the institution doing the study to take action internally to apply what it has learned. Discovering better ways to do things—and then rejecting them in favor of the old, traditional, comfortable ways—is an all-too-common conclusion, and benchmarking is a costly mistake if an organization is neither ready nor willing to change its old ways. Because organizational behavior depends on interlocking systems—the personnel system, the resource allocation system, the reward system, the communication system, and so on—adopting a best practice often requires far-reaching changes in an institution. Experienced organizations and their leaders never underestimate the difficulty of successfully implementing any change.

The benchmarking team must reveal the results it has discovered and "sell" the process to the institution; this requires that an institution achieve consensus on revised goals, establish action plans capable of achieving these goals, implement the plans, and monitor their results. None of this happens overnight. Finding and benefiting from a best practice may take months or years.

Once the changes gleaned from a benchmarking study have been implemented, an institution must recalibrate its own measures. It is not uncommon for an organization to discover its performance in a particular process has now improved to the point where its internal metrics are no longer sensitive to performance changes and consequently no longer serve to indicate future possible improvements. (The academic equivalent is grade inflation; if everyone's performance rates an "A," the incentive to work harder to excel may disappear.)

Processes for Higher Education to Benchmark

Once a college or university begins to view itself in process terms, the potential list of benchmarking targets begins to grow. An institution must select a process crucial to its mission and most likely to benefit its students and other stakeholders *if* improvements can be identified and adopted. Developing ideas for benchmarking typical business processes in an institution is usually easy. But an institution can also investigate best practices for how it might:

- augment its graduation/retention rates;
- broaden students' awareness and interests;

- develop and improve its curriculum;
- encourage desirable character traits;
- enrich the preparation of applying or accepted students;
- improve students' motivation to study;
- increase student and faculty understanding and use of technology;
- heighten student involvement in cocurricular activities;
- encourage students to study more (i.e., spend more "time on task");
- improve regular class attendance;
- engage its students intellectually;
- enrich out-of-class student interactions;
- develop good student work habits;
- promote library use;
- help its students learn more;
- improve placement/advising services;
- involve employers and other stakeholders in the design of academic programs and courses;
- keep expectations for student achievement high;
- maintain teachers' intellectual vitality;
- promote better teaching;
- provide transcripts that better reflect the skills, attitudes, and knowledge that most interest employers;
- raise faculty/staff morale and job satisfaction; or
- teach students to work cooperatively.

Best-practice benchmarking can be one time, periodic, or continual. It can contribute to strategic planning, forecasting, program/process comparisons (such as program review), and goal setting, or it can simply be one source for new ideas. The search for best practices can be external—gathering ideas from other organizations—or internal. In internal benchmarking, the goal is to articulate internal standards, share information, identify the best internal practices as a starting point, and encourage employees to communicate across organizational boundaries.

Closely related to best-practice benchmarking is competitive benchmarking, used to position an organization (and its products or services) relative to the marketplace. It often relies heavily on gathering from customers information on what makes them choose or prefer one product over another. Colleges typically conduct surveys or focus groups with applicants, matriculated students, and nonenrollees to gather this sort of information.

A Little Common-Sense Advice

Identifying "peer" institutions and gathering comparative data are relatively simple forms of benchmarking that help position an institution to see where gaps exist between its current performance and what might be possible. Benchmarking other organizations (in higher education or elsewhere) to discover best practices that might be transferred back to one's own institution is an expensive, demanding activity. To do this sort of benchmarking successfully, a college or university must first clearly understand the structure and performance of its *current* processes and systems. This internal analysis is itself a time- and resource-consuming task, but it remains a prerequisite for effective process benchmarking.

Suppose, for example, a college (or a North Central Association [NCA] evaluation team) identifies the process for curriculum review as needing attention—a "concern" or a "challenge." Before it benchmarks others' curriculum review processes, the college first needs to chart out every step in its current process and collect information on how those involved in the process comprehend the purpose of each procedure and its contribution to the overall goal (or goals) of the process. Commonly, when a college goes through such an analysis, it discovers unnecessary steps, cumbersome delays, and contradictory understandings about a process's purpose. Some may see curriculum review as a quest to provide the best instructional services for students, others as the means to avoid departmental rivalries (or to exploit them), still others as a means of keeping administrators employed. Unless there exists a *shared* recognition of the goals of a process, attempts to improve it—by benchmarking or any other means—are likely to be futile.

Once a process is clearly understood, a college then needs to measure the process's performance, outcomes, or results. "What you can't measure you can't improve" remains good advice. If a curriculum review process results in all reviewed courses continuing unchanged—the same results that would have been achieved if there were *no* process—then the process clearly adds nothing of value, and any investment of people's time, energies, and so on into curriculum review represents *waste*. On the other hand, if measures indicate that the process improves the resulting courses (measured, for example, by greater alumni satisfaction, increased learning, or lowered costs) or it improves morale and commitment to a set of shared values by the faculty and administration who participate in the process, those may be crucially important facts in deciding whether the process needs to be a conscious target for improvement and, if so, what characteristics the college should search for in identifying benchmarking partners.

Sadly, few higher education institutions are positioned to benefit from external best-practice benchmarking. Consequently they would be wise first to turn their attention to documenting, understanding, and measuring the performance of processes as they now exist. Only after they know where *they* stand can an institution's faculty and staff fruitfully search for peers, comparative data, benchmarking targets, and best practices.

RESOURCES TO LEARN MORE ABOUT BENCHMARKING

Consulting Firms

A variety of publications and videos about benchmarking are available from benchmarking consulting firms' websites. Most of these firms focus on benchmarking best practices; these consulting firms also organize group benchmarking studies and publish the results:

- American Productivity and Quality Center (APQC), 123 North Post Oak Lane, Houston, TX 77024; telephone (713) 681-4020; http://www.apqc.org
- The Benchmarking Network, Inc., 4606 FM 1960 West, Suite 300, Houston, TX 77069-9949; telephone (281) 440-5044; http://www.well.com/user/benchmar/tbnhome.html
- The Benchmarking Exchange (TBE), 7960-B Soquel Drive, Suite 356, Aptos, CA 95003; telephone (800) 662-9800; http://www.benchnet.com

Summaries of only APQC studies are available to nonmembers but can be downloaded from the website. APQC also conducts workshops teaching benchmarking techniques.

Books

Each of the following publications contains a good bibliography.

Alstete, Jeffrey W. *Benchmarking in Higher Education: Adapting Best Practices to Improve Quality*. ASHE-ERIC Higher Education Report No. 5 (1995). Washington, D.C.: The George Washington University Graduate School of Education and Human Development, 1995. This 141-page academic paperback provides an overview of the process of benchmarking for best practices, with numerous examples from higher education.

Camp, Robert C., ed. *Global Cases in Benchmarking: Best Practices from Organizations around the World*. Milwaukee: ASQ Quality Press, 1998. A 575-page compendium of case studies of benchmarking from around the world, edited by the principal of the Best Practices Institute, an internal research, education, and consulting organization focused on the capture, exchange, and adoption of best practice through benchmarking.

O'Dell, Carla, and C. Jackson Grayson Jr., with Nilly Essaides. *If Only We Knew What We Know: The Transfer of Internal Knowledge and Best Practice*. New York: The Free Press, 1998. A clear and lively book written for a broad, popular audience about best-practice benchmarking, relating it to the concept of the "learning organization," by two of the principals in the American Productivity and Quality Center.

Spendolini, Michael J. *The Benchmarking Book*. New York: American Management Association, 1992. A fine, older book that covers a variety of approaches to benchmarking.

Stewart, Thomas A. *Intellectual Capital: The New Wealth of Organizations*. New York: Doubleday, 1997. A best-selling popular book that deals with both internal and external best-practice benchmarking as a source of organizational value.

5

THE PRESENT STATE OF HIGHER EDUCATION

William Pepicello

"Reformers have the idea that change can be achieved by brutal sanity."

—George Bernard Shaw

Higher education in America is ripe for change. It stands as a monolith in a dynamic, rapidly evolving society in which access to information has been democratized through technological innovation and in which traditional notions of teaching/learning are no longer relevant to students whose approach to education is pragmatic as much as idealistic. Large impersonal lecture classes that embody the worst of what we know about how knowledge is transmitted and absorbed contrast sharply with the rest of a student's experience with the world, which the Internet has made highly personalized. If Amazon can employ a platform that adapts to its users and anticipates their preferences, why can't educational platforms? If banks can provide the convenience of self-service for basic transactions, why can't local colleges and universities? If Google and Wikipedia can provide access to information (albeit uneven in quality), why can't our education system provide immediate access to authentic knowledge?

In short, traditional higher education must adapt to society and abandon the outdated myth that knowledge is a hidden truth to be revealed by faculty to the benighted masses. Knowledge is everywhere, and we must now provide responsible and accountable access to it or be prepared for students to find that access elsewhere. It is this litany of shortfalls that has led to the current calls for access, accountability, transparency, and affordability, as first articulated in the Spellings Report (Spellings, 2006). Certainly the current infrastructure of American higher education, which is grounded in elitist tradition, has led in large part to the alarming decline of the United States in the ranking of educated countries in the world. The current system is geared toward educating a select group of the population who can then lead the nation. This model no longer reflects how our society functions, yet we persist in perpetuating it to the detriment of the country and to the continuing demise of the middle class.

Our society has become diverse and diversified. Only about 27 percent of undergraduate students in the United States now experience a "traditional" education whereby they enter a residential institution directly from high school and attend school full time. The other 73 percent, who we might call next-generation learners, are often older, first-generation students who are working and have family obligations. In the face of this fundamental shift in the nature of our student population, higher education has remained relatively stagnant and geared to a way of life that no longer represents the norm.

HOW IS INNOVATION FOSTERED IN THIS CLIMATE?

The key element in fostering innovation is accepting the inevitable, namely that the current system is not sustainable. It is not viable either as a vehicle for disseminating knowledge nor as a model of fiscal responsibility and stability. Openness to alternatives then must ensue in a way that allows for "out-of-the-box" thinking. Perhaps most importantly, this openness to change must engender a proactive approach to reform. We must stop talking and start doing.

This, of course, begs the question "Start doing what?" and in answering this question, we can find the guide to the future. We must start refocusing (or perhaps truly focus for the first time) on the student as the center of our education system. Our current infrastructure is designed for the convenience and comfort of institutions, faculty, and administration. It does not take into account who the students are, how they think, or what they need from higher education today. Nor does it ask. Further, it does not take account of the multiple resources available for student support and curricular enhancement that can enrich the education experience.

We must not just acknowledge but embrace technology as a partner in the education enterprise. In so doing, we must be prepared for new ways of investing resources—both human and fiscal—that do not fit the traditional paradigm. In short, we must be prepared to change attitudes and ultimately to transform the infrastructure of higher education.

CHALLENGES

There is less debate over what should and must be done than there is over the innumerable obstacles to be overcome. The list is both predictable and pedestrian. From my perspective, perhaps the most pernicious problem is simple inertia, comfort with the status quo and the "cottage industry" nature of higher education in which individual faculty members are seen as the repository of knowledge that they then transmit to students. This is a system built on self-interest that is threatened by the democratized model of education that dares to suggest that learning outcomes ought to be comparable across individual faculty members' classes, internally across academic programs, or even across institutions. Again, this model runs counter to the rest of an individual's larger life experience in which efficacy, and indeed quality, are expected to be comparable elements in any given sector.

More to the point, the current system must be evaluated and its outcomes assessed. This is a massive undertaking, rife with straw men. The most pervasive issue here is simple fear of innovation and opposition based on comfortable tradition. Let me offer a couple of self-serving examples. In 1989, the University of Phoenix made its first foray into the online world of education. For more than a decade, it was reviled and ridiculed in the higher education community, despite overwhelming success and affirmation from the most important constituency, its students. Today most colleges and universities offer a least some online instruction, and many see it as a way into the future. In the mid-1990s, the University of Phoenix sent waves through higher education by developing its virtual library, and by the early 2000s, it had extended this notion to textbooks and supporting educational resources for students. Again, this development met with great skepticism, despite the fact that materials could be delivered to students at a fraction of the cost of traditional channels. Today, one reads regularly about universities digitizing content.

The point here is that the challenge lies not in change per se but in the rational implementation of transformation in ways that allow for an evolutionary rather than a revolutionary execution. The investment of resources alluded to earlier, for example, need not entail a wholesale abandoning of existing systems and structures. Rather, as the University of Phoenix has demonstrated, innovation can be phased in to correspond to and mirror changes in student population, technology, and society in general. Such an approach, however, takes a much different attitude and much more engagement than we often find in the higher education community today.

It is important to point out that this is not change for the sake of change. Education must be integrated into the fabric of an individual's life in the same way as the banking example with which I began this piece. The very term *student* implies a separateness of the education enterprise that traditional higher education fosters and perpetuates. But in real life, designations like *worker*, *parent*, and indeed *student* now represent aspects of a seamless lifestyle in which these roles coexist simultaneously and fluidly rather than as individual and walled facets that are each distinct and separate in their essence. Education has lagged sadly behind in keeping up with the reality within which it exists.

One last major challenge to mention is the current factionalism of higher education. Too much is made of artificial or irrelevant differentiations of institutions, for example public versus private or not for profit versus for profit. We fail to see that higher education must exist as a set of alternative paths that enables a diverse society to achieve its education goals in diverse ways. We tend to ignore the complementary nature of internal higher education sectors, influenced by territoriality and self-interest. We obscure and eventually lose sight of basic issues like quality by focusing on the wrong indicators. For example, there is nothing inherently insidious about a for-profit business model in higher education. In fact, the for-profit model often leads to greater accountability and increased emphasis on issues of quality. I point in this regard to the Academic Annual Report that the University of Phoenix publishes in the spirit of transparency and accountability.

Essential issues are too often obscured by the fact that the for-profit sector is frequently treated as a "one-size-fits-all" segment that encompasses everything from unaccredited mom-and-pop enterprises to regionally accredited institutions that are held to the highest standards of educational quality by their peers. Matters of quality cannot genuinely be discussed generically across such a disparate sector any more than we would compare similar issues across two- and four-year institutions whose missions may vary dramatically. Rather than dwelling on faux differences and red herring arguments, higher education needs to establish a simple baseline of quality and then from that baseline build a new system that draws upon the strength of the complementary roles that the various types of institutions play. In short, higher education constituencies need to listen and act cooperatively to achieve one common and noble goal—the education of our populace.

WHERE FROM HERE?

The frustration in all this is that higher education knows that it must innovate and in many respects has grudgingly acknowledged key elements that will inform and guide that innovation: technology, a rededication to student success, and the democratization of knowledge, to name a few. Although the final destination may be hazy yet, we can see it. The problem lies in how we will get there. The path is not an easy one, but as with all journeys, it must be approached one step at a time. Many institutions are taking halting steps, some are lurching forward, and a few are actually striding into the future. We must all support each other and advance as a unified sector by sharing not just best practices but practices that will redefine higher education.

It is dismaying, but not surprising, to note at this point that observations about the ripe climate for innovation and the opportunities for nurturing innovation are far overshadowed by the list of challenges. We have the resources but not a common will to go where we must go. Well, nobody said it was easy. But perhaps the call to action lies in the fact that innovation, in my opinion, comes best from within. Higher education has the opportunity to innovate or, perhaps more accurately, to catch up with the rest of society. The innovation is all about us. We need only adapt it to our own purposes—before someone else does it for us.

6

COMMUNITY COLLEGES

Developing a Culture of Innovation and Change
Linda M. Thor

"Creativity is thinking up new things. Innovation is doing new things."

—Theodore Levitt

COMMUNITY COLLEGES AS DISRUPTIVE INNOVATIONS

Where should the search commence to locate best practices in academic innovation? Many opinion shapers would likely cite the role of universities as providers of research and development, sponsors of think tanks, and cultivators of knowledge expansion through theses and dissertations. What may be overlooked is the entrepreneurial spirit that resides in full measure within the nation's nearly 1,200 community colleges. They represent a distinctly American phenomenon. Birthed in 1901 at Joliet, Illinois, community colleges radically altered conventional wisdom by boldly affirming that higher education could and should not be a privilege but a right available to everyone.

Public community colleges originated as an affordable solution for local populations who did not have the means or desire to leave their home communities in order to pursue learning at universities. Disruptive innovations, according to Harvard Business School professor

Clayton Christensen (2008), are unexpected innovations that apply a different set of values to create new and unforeseen markets. By opening their doors to the masses, these new models became the most disruptive innovation in the prior five hundred years of higher education. Freed from the mandate to follow tradition and minus a mission to engage in formal research, community colleges reinvented how the learning experience was delivered, first in liberal arts and later in general education and occupational programs. Throughout their history, these colleges have continued to be responsive to their local communities through their student-centered approaches in access, services, and programs.

THE NEED FOR AN ORGANIZATIONAL CULTURE THAT IS CHANGE ADEPT

Now fast forward to the complexities of the twenty-first–century global marketplace. Community colleges serve 11.5 million learners annually—more than all U.S. universities combined. Their rapid response time positions them as ideal incubators for next-generation discoveries. However, the pressure is on all academic institutions to increase the number of degree completers. The competition for students among public and private colleges has intensified. More than ever, administrators must seek a balance between decreasing government revenues and increasing programs and services for diverse student populations. How does any institution, whether public or private, community college or university, find sufficient time and resources to nurture a spirit of innovation amid such a deadline-driven, politically charged atmosphere?

The answer is found in formulating an organizational culture that focuses systemwide on becoming entrepreneurial and change adept. Innovation and change are inexorably linked together. This chapter describes how the intentional development of such a culture can lead to innovations that positively impact every aspect of the college, from student success to employee engagement. Eric Shinseki, U.S. secretary of veterans' affairs and retired U.S. Army chief of staff, has often stated, "If you don't like change, you will like irrelevance even less" (cited in

Dao and Shanker 2009). This thought is profound whether it is applied to the military, a global corporation, a mom-and-pop business, or an institute of higher education.

DEFINING INNOVATION'S ROLE IN COMMUNITY COLLEGES

In surveying ten years of community college innovations across the country, O'Banion and Weidner (2009), with support from the MetLife Foundation, sought a consensus on the definition of *innovation*. In their 2009 national survey of community colleges, which received the Innovation of the Year Award from the League for Innovation in the Community College, educators surveyed chose to define *innovation* as the "creation of new opportunities that are transformative." Equal preference was given to the "development or adoption of new or existing ideas for the purpose of improving policies, programs, practices or personnel" (O'Banion and Weidner, 2009). As this chapter explores, there is tremendous value in looking outside academia for concepts that are transferable to education. Prolific management author Peter Drucker (2004), for example, thought of innovation as the path to wealth for business and the path to service and serving students for education.

In an example from the world of science, Thomas Edison stands tall as both innovator and inventor. Although he held more than one thousand patents in his name, he also experienced some notorious failures, including the rejection of his electronic machine that instantly tallied votes by legislators. He swiftly discovered there was no market for his invention because legislators thrived on the political process of lobbying and last-minute vote changes. After this disappointment Edison decided he would "never waste time inventing things that people would not want to buy" (Gelb and Miller Caldicott, 2008, p. 25). At first glance those words hardly seem applicable to academe, yet they have everything to do with the fact that today's student assumes a consumer mentality when selecting a college or university of choice. Our priority needs to stay focused on developing innovations that provide added value to students' college and university experiences.

MOTIVATORS BEHIND A SYSTEMIC
APPROACH TO INNOVATION

Most would agree that individual ingenuity occurs regularly in the form of motivated faculty members who regularly initiate programs and methods to benefit students. However, a majority of these learning enhancements are difficult to replicate, if only because they lack widespread access and recognition. What is less understood is how to create a more pervasive learning environment that encourages systemic innovation and change in order to increase student success. While the word *innovation* carries positive connotations, the idea of change itself is seldom welcomed. The perpetually quotable Drucker (2004) also stated, "One cannot manage change. One can only be ahead of it. . . . Unless it is seen as the task of the organization to lead change, the organization will not survive. In a period of rapid structural change, the only ones who survive are the change leaders. A change leader sees everything as an opportunity" (p. 335). Thus survival is a major impetus for colleges to head into uncharted territory. Change may also be prompted by dissatisfaction; a sense that business as usual isn't happening the way it once did. But change does not have to be rooted in failure or impending loss. At its best, it can be sought by reasonably thriving organizations that make a commitment to relentless improvement in order to accomplish their vision and mission and as a response to changing demographics.

Another strong motivator might be a desire to move "from good to great." Leaders may be compelled to better understand the entire system's issues through a wider lens. The college, perhaps prompted by an upcoming reaccreditation visit, might recognize that it needs to move from mere problem solving to a solution-centered mindset, as Edison would phrase it. Organizations that place a premium on student success may move forward based on the desire to more strongly identify with students' wants and needs. Or the college might want to become more forward thinking by exploring future opportunities to grow its existing markets.

Interestingly, the O'Banion and Weidner (2009) ten-year survey concluded that the majority of League for Innovation honorees were faculty driven and student centered as opposed to program driven.

Nearly one out of three received no financial backing from the institution or from grants.

THE RELATIONSHIP BETWEEN CULTURE STATEMENTS AND SYSTEMIC CHANGE

My personal interest and passion for systemic innovation stem from more than three decades of service in higher education, most of it in an entrepreneurial setting. From my vantage as both a long-time community college president and currently as a chancellor, I have acted in accordance with the belief that the road to educational innovation is paved by designing, implementing, and reinforcing an organizational culture rooted in a strong mission and vision of service.

However, just about every educational institution maintains culture statements, which may include statements of mission, vision, values, core practices, and more. The overarching factor common to those organizations that achieve greatness through systemic innovation is their ability to live out their culture statements by adopting a collegewide framework that promotes collaboration; the study and application of best practices from outside academia; and an investment in employees through hiring, training, communication, and rewards. During my twenty-year presidency, Rio Salado College in Tempe, Arizona, turned these best practices into lessons learned. As a result, Rio Salado transformed itself from a college of second choice to one of the nation's largest community colleges in headcount, serving more than 62,000 students annually through learning formats that include online, accelerated, and customized partnerships with business and industry.

Now as the new chancellor of the Foothill–De Anza Community College District in the Silicon Valley of California, I am studying the unique cultures of two large colleges with a significant history of innovation and leadership. Today Foothill and De Anza Colleges are lauded for exemplary practices in basic skills education, sustainability and environmental studies, open educational resources, civic engagement, teacher technology training, and international education, among other programs and services for unique student bodies.

INNOVATION AS A CONTINUOUS PROCESS

Innovation is a continuous process of improvement and not a moment in time or a satisfying brainstorm session. As Collins (2001) espouses in the bestseller *Good to Great: Why Some Companies Make the Leap and Others Don't*, "Everyone looks for the 'miracle moment' when 'change happens.' But ask the good-to-great executives when change happened. They cannot pinpoint a single key event that exemplified their successful transition."

Nor does the innovation realm belong exclusively to right-brain thinkers. Can innovation be practiced daily, even taught? Emphatically, yes. It can be learned and practiced systemically by all. Just reference Edison's more than two thousand meticulous notebooks that recorded his team's ideas, successes, and failures. He left a legacy of systematic innovation through five innovation competencies that can be studied and practiced by educators and executives alike (Gelb and Miller Caldicott, 2008). Edison was anything but the stereotype of the lone inventor who toiled away in his garage. He was a visionary with a strategic method for innovation through collaboration. Edison's Menlo Park lab was a hotbed of daily research, learning, and teamwork that led to nearly 1,100 successful patents.

THE TRANSFORMATION OF RIO SALADO COLLEGE, TEMPE, AZ

The lessons learned by Rio Salado College as it adopted a culture of innovation and change are duplicable for those community colleges and universities that can look beyond tradition. Established organizations are seldom afforded the luxury of rebuilding their culture from the ground up. Nor do many of them desire to do so. Fortunately, I received that opportunity in 1990 when I arrived on the scene as the newly installed president of Rio Salado, a nontraditional community college founded in 1978 as a "college without walls." While its origin was steeped in innovation, more than a decade later its decentralized structure made it difficult to realize economies of scale, and the autonomy of multiple sites resulted in a college that was internally competitive.

Resources were austere. In fact, the college's very survival was at stake on a year-to-year basis.

However, after purposefully undergoing dramatic systemic change to its culture between 1990 and 2000, Rio Salado became the most cost-effective of the ten colleges in the Maricopa Community College District. Its reputation reversed from a "college of second choice" to a "college of first choice" for students. Double-digit growth in headcount became the norm. A culture of innovation and change that once appeared to be an impossible dream is still intact two decades after the college determined to reinvent itself. On employee engagement surveys, the staff now assigns high scores to statements such as "I understand how my job supports Rio's mission." What factors led to such transformational change? And can those factors be found at play in large traditional colleges where cultures within cultures exist, consensus building can be difficult, and "rocking the boat" isn't always welcome?

LESSON LEARNED #I: ADOPT A FLEXIBLE FRAMEWORK TO SHAPE A CULTURE BY DESIGN

According to the Disney Institute (2001), which has trained millions of executives over a twenty-five–year period, every institution has a culture, whether it is intentional or accidental. In the early 1990s, Rio Salado set in motion the foundational tools that launched the process of intentionally shaping its culture by design rather than by default. It realized what was needed first was a framework that would unify employees across the board for common goals, and that initial framework became the principles of total quality management (TQM). All employees received extensive training in TQM and were encouraged to apply their knowledge in meetings. This contributed to the adoption of a common vocabulary, such as "plan-do-check-act." Together, employees began to focus intently on improving processes.

As the president and the one who introduced the college to TQM, I was visible from the start in leading the way by example, along with the rest of the college's senior administrators and faculty chairs. When employees observe the executive team's hands-on involvement and enthusiasm for new initiatives, they are far more likely not only to accept changes but to jump on the bandwagon. For several years, TQM aligned with the college's strategy to incorporate quality into its culture. In its third year of TQM implementation, Rio Salado became the only educational institution to receive the Arizona Governor's Award for Quality—the coveted Pioneer Award. However, after a few years, the college also experienced limitations within the TQM framework. For example, meetings sometimes became overly focused on semantics and tools. In time, the college concluded that adhering too closely to a single framework had become restrictive. Therefore, college leaders made a conscious decision to retain the best of TQM, but a search was launched for a different type of framework—one that would allow the college to transition to a higher level of innovative thinking. They found a perfect match while studying Senge's (1990) principles as described in *The Fifth Discipline*, an organizational development book that describes the qualities of learning organizations. Senge's disciplines include personal mastery, mental models, shared vision, and team learning. But it was the fifth discipline, systems thinking, that would ultimately have the most impact upon the evolution of the college culture. Systems thinking is a blueprint for how organizations can innovate and change through integrating all aspects of the college. In systems thinking, the performance of the whole is greater than the capabilities of its individual parts. When systems thinking is consistently practiced with the other disciplines, the end result is a learning organization—one in which lifelong learning becomes second nature to the employees.

Changing the focus from TQM to the principles of the learning organization was a paradigm shift that ultimately empowered Rio Salado to more clearly articulate the college's mission and unusual vision statements: For most of the past decade, the college's vision statement has been "We astonish our customers!" In another example, as Rio Salado prepared to offer its first online courses in 1996, it drew upon systems thinking to reject a "distance learning department" that operated as a silo. Instead, the entire college would utilize an integrated approach to support online teaching and learning. Senge's learning organization principles also strengthened Rio Salado's focus on implementing innovation and change through the involvement of leaders at every level. According to Senge (1990), a shared vision occurs when leaders, faculty and staff have a similar picture and are committed to everyone having it: "Few if any, forces in human affairs are as powerful as a shared vision" (p. 192).

The roots of the culture and shared vision in the Foothill–De Anza District can be traced back to its founders, the original board of trustees, and early administrators who were uncompromising in their insistence upon access with excellence, hiring only the most qualified faculty and staff, and building beautiful and functional campuses. And located in the heart of the Silicon Valley, the spirit of innovation that flourishes in startup and established businesses alike is reflected in its community colleges that consistently outpace peers in measures of student success. Its cultural framework is shared governance, the power to engage numerous stakeholders, and the innovation that emanates from doing so.

LESSON LEARNED #2: CROSS-FUNCTIONAL COLLABORATION IS ESSENTIAL TO SYSTEMIC SUCCESS

Of the 173 innovations in the aforementioned O'Banion and Weidner (2009) survey, perhaps the biggest surprise concerned the degree to which the innovators collaborated. Teams as opposed to individuals developed a full 85 percent of the honored innovations. Although many of those teams consisted of no more than three individuals, more than three fourths of the recipients stated that their innovation was better for being the product of collaboration rather than individual effort. Individuals achieve pockets of change, and that is admirable; however, systemic innovation that permanently impacts the entire organizational culture is most likely to result from teamwork and partnerships.

The Rio Salado approach to innovation through collaboration is inclusive rather than exclusive. Teams are cross-functional across multiple employee groups and interdisciplinary among faculty. What's more, faculty and senior administrators are in close physical proximity and frequently consult with each other, for example, in training sessions and through relentless improvement teams. Teams may be both internal and external. An example of internal collaboration is the Rio Salado Development Team, formed as the college's internal think tank. The cross-functional team consists of senior administrators, faculty chairs, and staff from such functions as marketing. Over the years its role has enlarged from that of process improver to driver of innovation, such as when the college decided to implement fifty annual start dates for its online courses.

An example of an external educational partnership that resulted in a significant technology innovation occurred when 120 Rio Salado employees teamed with Microsoft consultants over a two-year period for research and development. The resulting product is the college's highly customized online learning management system, named RioLearn. It should be noted that full-time faculty had a high level of hands-on involvement in its development and were given time and resources to accomplish this. Within the Foothill–De Anza Community College District, one of the most unique multidisciplinary "classrooms" is De Anza College's Euphrat Museum of Art that features contemporary exhibits focusing on political, social, and historic issues. The museum is about collaboration—collaboration between artists; collaboration with students and instructors; and collaboration among artists, students, and the community. For example, the same exhibit can provide opportunities to learn how to think differently and how to further discussion for students of sociology, communication, humanities, as well as art.

LESSON LEARNED #3: BORROW BEST PRACTICES FROM EXTERNAL INFLUENCERS

An important factor leading to innovation is that sufficient resources are allocated in the form of time, finances, and space. A tremendous strength of learning organizations is they are empowered to look externally for best practices utilized by business and by consortiums of educational leaders. Rio Salado College has derived enormous value in adopting such concepts as customer astonishment, good-to-great organizations, and blue-ocean thinking from business bestsellers. To broaden its circle of external influencers, Rio Salado became one of thirteen founding members of the Continuous Quality Improvement Network (CQIN). This national alliance of community college leaders serves as a forum for educators to become learning partners. At summer institutes CQIN team members have studied organizational sustainability with Toyota and the importance of culture statements at Saturn, learned the principles of legendary service from Ritz-Carlton, and analyzed team dynamics at Edison's Menlo Park lab. These annual site visits reinforce that innovation is a team process that can be unilaterally learned and is not just about "doing things differently."

As a result of a CQIN Institute that featured Steelcase and IDEO, a Palo Alto design and innovation firm, Rio Salado's faculty created unique collaborative workspaces in its new administrative and faculty center. The unusual configuration encourages constant interaction and avoids silos. As an example, Internet-friendly seating arrangements called "front porches" are located just outside the offices of full-time faculty. These collaborative spaces became the only educational innovation in the nation to earn top honors in the 2009 Edison Best New Product Awards Competition/Living and Working Environments Category.

External influencers are regularly invited to share best practices in the Foothill–De Anza District. For forty-three years Foothill's Celebrity Forum hosted such speakers as Tony Blair, Thomas Friedman, David Brooks, and Yo-Yo Ma. Similarly Foothill's Entrepreneurship Center and De Anza's Institute for Community and Civic Engagement simultaneously "pull in" and "reach out" to external influencers.

LESSON LEARNED #4: CULTIVATE EMPLOYEE DEVELOPMENT PROGRAMS THAT REINFORCE THE CULTURE

Colleges that purposefully live out their mission and vision also understand the difficulty in sustaining their culture without widespread employee buy-in. Therefore, any strategies to strengthen the organization's culture must include effective employee development. As a learning organization with a strong focus on systems thinking, Rio Salado has long practiced a four-pronged approach to employee development, and it begins with the hiring process.

For hiring nonfaculty positions, positive attitude and motivation trump specific degrees earned. Rio Salado learned from its external partners at IDEO to search for and hire T-shaped people, that is, those who have potential for professional growth in both width and breadth (Kelly and Littman, 2001). Interviews with prospective employees focus not only on skills-sets and managerial abilities but also on finding individuals who have the greatest potential for making successful contributions. Rio Salado's hiring teams seek those most likely to identify with the Rio mission and vision and who can grasp systems thinking. The edge goes to candidates who can project passion, goals, optimism, and the ability to persist—all vital to a healthy organizational culture.

Another important element for a climate of innovation is to integrate all employee groups during training. New hires should not be left alone to figure out the organization's culture for themselves. Rio Salado developed an extensive modular training program called "The Rio Way" taught by teams of leaders at every level. Employees are immersed in Rio's history, culture, mission, and vision. They gain a common vocabulary, such as the importance of shared vision and mental models. Fear is removed, and newer employees learn they are valued. Perhaps the most significant end result is that employees learn in a systematic way how their individual roles contribute to the organization as a whole through systems thinking. Other customized training programs include Leaders Managing the Rio Way, to improve communication and supervisory skills, and StrengthsQuest, which helps employees identify and cultivate their natural talents (Anderson and Clifton, 2002).

Finally, employee development is fostered through an employee-driven rewards and recognition program. Rather than have college leadership bestow honors such as "employee of the month," any employee can nominate any other employee for a job well done in teamwork, relentless improvement, customer focus, sustainability, inclusiveness, or professionalism. Honorees receive a departmental visit from the president, a letter of commendation for their personnel files, an icon for their personal awards plaque, and their choice of gifts from college merchandise.

Employee development at Foothill and De Anza Colleges that reinforces the culture include reading and reflection programs in which a group reads the same book and reflects together on the implications. Examples are *Other People's Children: Cultural Conflict in the Classroom* (Delpit, 2006) as a vehicle to discuss racism and bias, *Tribes: We Need You to Lead Us* (Godin, 2008) to discuss giving everyone a chance to lead, and *Drive: The Surprising Truth about What Motivates Us* (Pink, 2009) to discuss motivations and rewards. A new districtwide "peak performance" training program for administrators and supervisors is designed to improve institutional effectiveness and individual performance. The monthly training sessions address topics ranging from ethics, communication, and teams to emerging diversity issues and cultural competence, research and technology tools, and sharing best practices.

CONCLUSIONS

While the contributions of individuals will always play a significant role in student success, twenty-first–century educational institutions primarily require systemic innovation, made possible through a change-adept culture. Community colleges, founded as disruptive innovations with open doors, are ideally suited to innovate because of their rapid responsiveness and student-centered focus. After determining which framework works best for their mission and vision, community colleges can learn to shape their culture by design through cross-functional teams, implementation of external best practices, and employee development that enhances engagement.

II

SUCCESS

In Their Own Words
Allan M. Hoffman

According to the Spellings Report, "American higher education has become what, in the business world, would be called a mature enterprise: increasingly risk-averse, at times self-satisfied, and unduly expensive" (Spellings, 2006, p. ix). A "mature enterprise" is often prone to entrenchment in the status quo and can get mired in a morass of hierarchical protocols. Untried approaches to old conundrums appear fraught with risk. Self-satisfaction impedes the rapid adoption of change, and cost concerns inhibit openness to good-faith gambles of unproven potential. It was not always so. In earlier days, society looked to institutions of higher learning to define fresh knowledge, create new systems, and invent novel processes. Colleges and universities routinely proposed the initial theory, endeavored to prove it through research, and presented their final verdicts to students as irrefutable truths. In the 1960s and 1970s, social critique and political debate began to question the role of tertiary institutions as sole developers of cutting-edge protocols and solutions. Increased state and federal scrutiny in the 1980s contracted the focus of higher education to defending the effectiveness of data transfer and curricular value. Higher education confined its emphasis to discovering new knowledge, often without risking the impact of its implications or applications. With the introduction of new theories on "flattened management" and the widespread adoption of process improvement methodologies, the business sector took the lead in innovative approaches. Higher education resorted to the relative safety of proposing theoretical models and modes of practice, assessing their effectiveness in real-world use, and documenting or credentialing these processes as a part of business partnership models.

Everett M. Rogers (1995) states that innovation is related not only to new knowledge but also to the decision to adopt it. He speaks to the "diffusion of innovations" and defines it as the "process by which an innovation is communicated through certain channels over a period of time among the members of a social system." An innovation is an "idea, practice, or object that is perceived to be new by an individual or other unit of adoption. . . . Communication is a process in which participants create and share information with one another to reach a mutual understanding" (Rogers, 1995). There is a renewed openness in higher education for exploring, attempting, and adopting unique and sometimes radical approaches to long-standing issues. With the encouragement of their leaders, staff and educators from all types of tertiary institutions are improving long-established approaches, piloting new systems, and performing innovative wonders. Through the sharing of these examples of more efficient process, improved practices, and more effective methods, the following chapters hope to foster and expand the "communication" phase of the diffusion process beyond their local scope.

7

ACADEMIC QUALITY MEASURES

The Academic Quality Improvement Program (AQIP),
The Higher Learning Commission, Chicago, Illinois
Stephen D. Spangehl

"Once we rid ourselves of traditional thinking we can get on with creating the future."

—James Bertrand

The Academic Quality Improvement Program (AQIP) is an alternative process through which an accredited college or university can maintain its status with the Higher Learning Commission. AQIP's goal is to infuse the principles and benefits of continuous improvement into the culture of colleges and universities in order to ensure and advance the quality of higher education—and to help institutions keep meeting any and all accreditation standards. AQIP allows an institution to demonstrate that it meets the Higher Learning Commission's criteria for accreditation and other expectations through processes that align with the ongoing activities that characterize institutions striving continuously to improve their performance. By sharing both its improvement activities and their results through AQIP, an institution develops the structure and systems essential to achieving the distinctive higher education mission it has set for itself—and the evidence to enable the commission to reaffirm accreditation.

AQIP was developed and launched in 1999 with a grant from the Pew Charitable Trusts. It has grown steadily from its original fourteen institutions in 2000–2001 to more than two hundred in 2010. Its website, www.AQIP.org, lists the number and names of current participants and provides full details about AQIP's strategy forums, systems appraisals, and various other services.

Based upon principles common to high-performance institutions, AQIP draws from a variety of initiatives and programs—total quality management (TQM), continuous improvement (CI), Six Sigma, ISO 9000 registration, state and national quality awards, and others. Many of AQIP's quality principles—focusing on key processes, basing decisions on data, decentralizing control, empowering faculty and staff to make the decisions that directly affect their work—have long been traditions in higher education, although their form and the breadth of their practice in particular institutions may vary greatly. Other components, such as systems thinking and stakeholder focus, appear at first to be new to academia but turn out to be in close alignment with the values and behaviors of higher educators. To provide a new process for maintaining accreditation, AQIP has created a new set of analytic categories, activities, and procedures that are different from those used in traditional accreditation while continuing to ensure that institutions meet the commission's criteria for accreditation.

What makes it most innovative is its separation of formative activities, all designed to help an institution improve the quality of its processes and performance, and its summative judgment on whether an institution meets accreditation standards. Traditionally, regional accreditation has combined both ends, quality assurance and quality improvement, attempting to achieve both using a single package of policies and processes. Accreditation's quality assurance function is a crucial one. Because maintaining accreditation is essential to participation in student aid programs, many institutions justifiably see accreditation processes as activities that can do much harm unless carefully managed. To many, the potential benefits—of critical introspection, of self-study, of peer review, of public accountability for the achievement of stated goals—pale when joined with an assurance process on which so much rides. Risk taking, no matter how highly praised elsewhere, is not attractive where accreditation is concerned.

AQIP disentangles assurance from improvement through the structure of the elements it expects institutions to follow. By separating the assurance and improvement agendas, AQIP—for the 90 percent or more of institutions where ensuring minimum levels of quality is not the primary issue—lowers the level of reaccreditation anxiety so that a serious and sustained focus on quality improvement can occur.

AQIP's "Principles of High Performance Organizations" (2010), which can be downloaded from the Higher Learning Commission website (www.ncahlc.org) as an Adobe PDF file, underlie all of AQIP's elements, activities, and procedures. They represent the values that participating colleges, universities, and AQIP itself strive to embody:

- a mission and vision that focus on serving students' and other stakeholders' needs;
- broad-based faculty, staff, and administrative involvement;
- leaders and leadership systems that support a quality culture;
- a learning-centered environment;
- respect for people and willingness to invest in them;
- collaboration and a shared institutional focus;
- agility, flexibility, and responsiveness to changing needs and conditions;
- planning for innovation and improvement;
- fact-based information gathering and thinking to support analysis and decision making; and
- integrity and responsible institutional citizenship

AQIP puts forward nine categories to help analyze and improve the systems essential to all effective colleges and universities. The name of each AQIP category refers to a group of related processes: "Helping Students Learn," "Accomplishing Other Distinctive Objectives," "Understanding Students' and Other Stakeholders' Needs," "Valuing People," "Leading and Communicating," "Supporting Institutional Operations," "Measuring Effectiveness," "Planning Continuous Improvement," and "Building Collaborative Relationships." For example, "Helping Students Learn" includes the largest group of crucial processes in higher education institutions, processes dealing with program and curricular design and delivery. Each category allows an institution to analyze, understand, and explore opportunities for improving these processes. Metaphorically, the categories serve as "buckets" that allow institutions to sort their key institutional processes into analyzable groups and as "lenses" that permit in-depth examination of each group of processes.

Categories identify specific issues (in the form of questions) that guide the institution in structuring its systems portfolio and in crafting action projects. The items in each category pose different types of questions: *process questions* that ask how an institution has designed and deployed processes that help it achieve its overall goals; *results questions* that ask about the performance of institutional processes, whether their performance results meet requirements of stakeholders; and *improvement questions* that ask how the institution promotes systemic improvement of its processes and performance in each category. Because each of the nine AQIP categories examines a set of processes vital to every college or university, the categories together are comprehensive, covering all of the key processes and goals found in any higher education institution. The AQIP categories' comprehensive nature and specific questions about processes, results, and improvement allow each institution to fully describe its activities and accomplishments while analyzing itself in a way that promotes critical and productive thinking about improvement.

When an institution using AQIP is required to provide evidence that it meets the commission's criteria for accreditation, it can usually reference the same evidence it provides in answering the AQIP category questions. AQIP also provides guides to illustrate the alignment between the commission's five criteria for accreditation and the AQIP categories. AQIP's core processes include strategy forums, action projects, annual updates, systems portfolios, systems appraisals, quality checkup visits, and reaffirmation of accreditation, which enables a college or university participating in AQIP to demonstrate its continued fulfillment of the commission's criteria for accreditation. Descriptions of each process can be found at the AQIP website. Reaffirmation of accreditation functions as the summative review for the quality assurance aspects of the evaluation but continues the formative evaluation that is a fundamental emphasis of AQIP.

The AQIP reaffirmation panel is assigned several institutions to review each year and conducts its work through a series of conference and e-mail exchanges. It examines each organization's current systems portfolio and its last six years of action projects, systems appraisals, and other interactions with AQIP and the commission, including reports of the quality checkup visit as well as any additional organizationally requested or commission-sponsored visits. The panel documents satisfactory evidence of compliance with each of the criteria for accreditation. In exceptional cases in which the evidence is incomplete, the panel seeks and obtains additional facts or verification before it makes a recommendation on continued accreditation to the Higher Learning Commission's Institutional Actions Council, which makes most of its accreditation decisions.

The following examples illustrate the successes of AQIP.

ACCREDITATION, QUALITY IMPROVEMENT, AND STRATEGY

Michael R. Chipps and Cinch L. Munson

Mid-Plains Community College (MPCC) has created a comprehensive vision for the college by tying comprehensive strategic planning to accreditation through AQIP from the North Central Association's Higher Learning Commission. This symbiotic planning approach links collectively developed crucial processes, specifically strategy, accreditation, and quality improvement, while respecting MPCC's core mission and values.

Since 2003, MPCC leadership has continued to be instrumental in developing and accomplishing the goals of more traditional three-year strategic plans, known as "Shaping Our Future." In 2008, a systemic change was in the making as the college applied for and was accepted into the Higher Learning Commission's AQIP. This acceptance happened to coincide with the college's 2009–2012 "Shaping Our Future." Like a revelation, it became crystal clear that this was an exclusive moment to unify accreditation, quality improvement, and strategic planning, all of which are mission crucial to the college yet had traditionally been separately developed and managed. It became evident that this convergence could be accomplished through AQIP.

Deciding to proceed with this innovative approach to planning did not take much additional contemplation, and with simple and ample communication, the preparation framework was developed with relative ease. One of the first major steps was to garner support of the college's governing board for the new planning concept. The governing board had historically participated in the development and approval of the strategic plan and had already taken a major step by adopting AQIP as the accreditation model for the college. The nine AQIP categories aligned well with the strategic priorities of previous "Shaping Our Future" plans, so the board readily endorsed the new strategic planning approach.

The AQIP core team reviewed previous strategic planning processes to identify opportunities for process improvement. The previous planning approach emphasized external stakeholder input leading to creating plans for each strategic initiative. To improve upon this process, an additional dimension was introduced to also incorporate internal input into the 2009–2012 comprehensive plan. Also, for each category the college would include tangible AQIP action projects to improve processes.

To identify possible strategic initiatives and action projects, the AQIP core team and college cabinet conducted idea generation workshops to identify possible strategic initiatives and action projects for the 2009–2012 comprehensive plan. For each AQIP category, cross-functional work groups were formed across the multicollege district. Each group brainstormed possible initiatives and action projects that could be undertaken to advance the institution. After a brainstorming period, each work group shared the ideas that were generated and explained the concept. All of the ideas were collected, documented in the original format for the next step in the process, and then incorporated into an online survey. Using the online survey, the AQIP core team and college cabinet were asked to identify the top five priority initiatives in each strategic AQIP category. This process narrowed the long list of "raw" ideas for each category to five concepts per category. The AQIP core team then put the five potential concepts into a format that could be readily communicated and understood via another online survey, which was e-mailed to all full-time college employees. Employees were asked to identify their top three priorities on the list, which resulted in three initiatives for each of the nine strategic AQIP categories. The final categories and planning initiatives were then presented to the MPCC board of governors for review, comment, and final approval. Following board approval, the college cabinet then identified a specific cabinet member to be accountable for each initiative. Cabinet members then worked with other college faculty and staff to establish goals, timelines, and responsibility for the completion of each initiative. As appropriate, project teams worked with the college AQIP core team to identify tangible action projects based on newly identified initiatives.

The marriage of strategic planning to accreditation and quality improvement with AQIP is of significant benefit to MPCC. Resources were used more effectively during the planning phase, and the multiple projects are all working toward similar important outcomes. Challenging institutional issues were effectively resolved using the collective power of those most affected by those processes. But, even more importantly, students benefit because processes that affect them are improved.

The overall benefit of aligning "Shaping Our Future" comprehensive planning with AQIP is yet to be realized, as it is still being developed and implemented. If it works appropriately, it will not reach capacity. The college has already realized increased efficiencies and continues to realize increased effectiveness by combining major planning and administrative operations. The comprehensive vision from this process draws collective attention from internal and external stakeholders to create a common focal point to meet students' and other stakeholders' needs. Strategic planning based on AQIP principles and joined with accountable leadership initiates and sustains meaningful initiatives and valuable AQIP action projects, thereby instilling an environment within the college that honors, respects, and exudes continuous quality improvement.

STRATEGIC ALIGNMENT AND MEASUREMENT

Dave Weber, Christine Miller, and Marilyn Hansmann

In an effort to align people, process, resources, and strategy with outcomes, Rochester Community and Technical College (RCTC) has developed a unique College Performance Improvement System (CPIS) via several interlocking processes, including strategic planning and an annual integrated planning process (IPP) linked with a balanced scorecard (BSC) approach. This improvement system fosters a culture focused on assessment, improvement, innovation, and evidence. Not unlike most colleges, RCTC used a historical strategic planning approach that first identified available resources before setting strategy. The new approach focuses first on desired outcomes, then assesses college strengths and opportunities, identifies strategy, and allocates resources. By addressing what defines college success first, the college can identify core measures to address the question "Are we successful?"

The Strategic Planning Process   RCTC adopted a multiphase strategic planning process (SPP) in 2000. Since that time, three cycles of SPP improvement have occurred. Currently the process has five phases, including landscape analysis (strengths, weaknesses, threats, and opportunities), signature review (mission, vision, and values), organizational analysis (AQIP, Baldrige Performance Excellence and Minnesota Quality Award assessment findings), process management (college work systems and key process), and identification of core measures and goals. The SPP is conducted every three years and guides longer-term planning. The principal focus of strategic planning is to start with the end in mind, that is, what will define our success as an institution, or which measures will demonstrate the accountability of the institution, student success, and our contribution to the community? The focus is on outcomes. Once the core measures representing desired outcomes are set, then goals are established. The improvement system then focuses on aligning and integrating people and processes to foster improvement, innovation, and student and stakeholder success and the achievement of goals.

The Balanced Scorecard (BSC)   The BSC is the second foundational component of CPIS. The BSC is a series of dashboards that cascade throughout every level of the college and includes the RCTC strategic dashboard, six divisional dashboards, and more than ninety academic program and service department dashboards. This dashboard system mirrors that of the Minnesota State Colleges and Universities Accountability Dashboard. RCTC publically launched its dashboard system in the fall of 2009. The intent was to create a culture of continuous improvement and evidence. If targets for identified core measures linked to strategies and goals are not being achieved, then a plan-do-check-act (PDCA) process is initiated to learn from the data to create positive change.

The College Strategic Dashboard includes forty-one core measures linked to thirteen goals around its four strategic priorities: access and opportunity, quality programs and services, meet state and regional economic needs, and innovation and efficiency. The dashboard uses a color-coded system to indicate the progress being made toward the strategic goals. Measures exceeding performance expectations are coded as gold, those meeting expectations as blue, and those in need of immediate attention as red. The color is determined by performance that is evaluated on three perspectives. The first is the trend in the data for that measure. The second perspective is performance against a comparative benchmark. The third perspective is performance to a target set for the measure. Measures have set tolerances that establish a basis for performance. Such tolerances may also be viewed as an error margin or standard deviation. The established tolerance is what causes the dials on the dashboard to move. Each measure has a dial for trend, comparative, and target. The performance for each is mathematically calculated based on tolerances set.

Each of the college's six divisions, including teaching and learning, student development and services, finance and facilities, strategic operations, human resources, and technology, have dashboards. These dashboards include strategies and core measures to track performance objectives that are linked to college goals. Division strategies are to be implemented over a one- or two-year timeframe. Division dashboards include core measures from the College Strategic Dashboard and others that are unique to the divisions' work.

Department dashboards include core measures from their division's dashboard and others that are unique to the department's work processes or to work performed by the department's division. Each department strategy includes actions and resources needed (if any) and then is linked to a defined work process and then a core measure for that process. All work is a process. All work can be measured. At division and department levels, the color coding reflects the overall performance for that core measure. Division and department dashboard performance is assessed based on preestablished tolerances and error margins for each measure. Program and department leaders can input contextual notes in their dashboards describing depicted performance, driver of performance, or what special causes might have contributed negative results.

The Integrated Planning Process (IPP) The third foundational component of CPIS is the annual IPP. Dashboard performance and other evaluative tools, such as accreditation, are then used to determine both strengths to leverage and opportunities for improvement.

All academic and service departments participate in the annual IPP, which has three major parts. The first is academic program review (APR) or service review (SR). This self-assessment step informs strengths, opportunities for improvement, and the development of continuous improvement plans. Second, continuous improvement plans are submitted via a Web-based portal and include strategy statements, action plans, resource requests (if needed), impacted processes, and core measures that define success. The department strategies cascade upward to their division strategies and then to college goals. Continuous improvement plan submissions focus on reprioritizing resources to new issues while discontinuing work on others. They also create a competitive pool of funds categorically established each year by the college. The third step of the IPP is the submission of operating budget requests.

Conclusion The design of these three interlocking processes creates mechanisms serving as the foundation of CPIS. This system ensures strategic alignment, fosters continuous innovation and improvement, and links people and process to goals, all in an environment focused on creating a culture of evidence.

SBARO AS A STANDARDIZED COMMUNICATION TOOL

Nancy S. Perryman and Patricia A. Stockert

SBARO (situation, background, assessment, recommendation, outcome/ownership) is a formal communication tool utilized at Saint Francis Medical Center's College of Nursing. Any committee or individual recommending a change or innovation, new policy, or new program completes an SBARO to communicate the data and the information in a formalized, standardized process. The SBARO ensures that data are used to validate purpose, problems, and recommendations and allow for a measurement of successful implementation of the policy put in place. SBARO stands for

- S = *situation:*
  - What is the situation?
  - Provide a concise statement of the problem.

- B = *background:*
  - What background information is pertinent to the situation?
  - Provide data whenever possible—a brief historical overview.
- A = *assessment:*
  - Based on the data, what do you think?
  - Provide analysis and consideration of options.
  - What is the cost?
- R = *recommendation*
  - What action/recommendation is needed to correct the problem?
  - Will this affect other areas of the college?
  - When will the action start?
  - Who will write the policy?
- O = *outcomes/ownership*
  - Was the recommendation approved?
  - Do the performance indicators verify the sustainability of the recommendations?
  - Who is the process/change owner?

Within the College of Nursing, faculty and staff have increased in size and numbers in the past several years. Since 2003, enrollment has grown from 221 to 498 master of science in nursing and bachelor of science in nursing students. Additionally, college employees have grown from fifty to seventy-two. As the college grew, communication between and among different offices became difficult and fragmented, which presented a challenge in knowing what was happening in each office. Previously the college made changes based on assumptions from employee/student survey feedback and not on supporting data. Change occurring in one office affected members in other offices. The group initiating the change may not have been aware of the impact in other areas.

SBARO originated in health care as a standardized reporting communication tool. OSF Saint Francis Medical Center has been using SBARO as a communication technique for about four years. SBARO is used to request FTEs (full time staff positions) to improve patient safety and patient care and communicate with physicians. Implementing SBARO at the college built continuity between the medical center and the college. Various offices (administration, admissions, student finance) were already successfully using the SBARO tool, however the college recognized that there was not a consistent mechanism for proposing and communicating change.

SBARO was a year-long AQIP project. The AQIP team researched different communication models and selected the SBARO as its recommendation. In May 2008, the SBARO tool was approved at the college senate as a pilot for the 2008–2009 academic year to be reviewed in May 2009.

The implementation phase occurred in several steps. We developed an SBARO policy and tool, which was revised twice as inconsistencies were addressed. We had two all-college meetings in order to educate employees in regard to SBARO. In addition, we developed a Power-Point presentation to provide a resource for new hires to learn what an SBARO is and how to write one. We added the outcomes/ownership section to the SBARO to be able to track the success and implementation of the policy that resulted from an SBARO. We are in the process now of developing an evaluation tool to be able to report back to administration on the use of the SBARO. In February 2010, we created an SBARO mandatory education unit, which is a required yearly review of SBARO for all employees.

The only cost to develop and implement SBARO was the time commitment of the committee while working on the project. Getting faculty and staff buy-in was challenging initially. The president set the standard that no changes or policies could be brought to the college senate without an SBARO. To meet this new standard, the AQIP committee, which is dedicated to quality improvement principles and processes, developed a policy for SBARO use. Once education and more discussion occurred, employees found that writing an SBARO was not as difficult as first imagined. Two clarifications were needed. The first was that an SBARO was not required to explore or develop a new idea. The exploration phase was needed to gather data to verify or support the problem situation. The SBARO brought the completed change or policy to the college senate or president for approval. A second clarification was that the proposed change had to clearly define the implementation and evaluation and identify a process owner to ensure sustainability.

There is no cost to operate and maintain the use of SBARO. SBARO has increased the efficiency of requesting change and reporting changes. Data, alternatives, and budgetary implications are presented as components of SBARO. The addition of the *O* identified an owner for the process to sustain and manage the change.

In order to measure and evaluate SBAROs, we have developed an SBARO table that tracks all the SBAROs written in an academic year. It contains data such as who wrote the SBARO, where it was presented (committee, supervisor, etc.), whether it was approved, effective date, current status, policy created, what was communicated, process owner, and evaluation process. This is an efficient way for us to measure the performance indicators and how we are using SBAROs. It was important for us to see how those changes are impacting our institution. The number of SBAROs written, how many were approved, and the results are tracked annually by the SBARO coordinator, who is the current associate dean of institutional research. The SBARO coordinator is also a resource to College of Nursing employees if they have any questions about the SBARO process.

Copies of the SBARO policy, template, SBARO flowchart, FAQ sheet, and an educational PowerPoint presentation are available to all employees on the shared computer drive. The SBARO is used to bring all new changes in processes, policies, or other decisions to the appropriate decision-making body, such as the college senate. SBAROs are also utilized within departments as changes in technology and processes evolve. SBARO helps the college make data-driven decisions and improve efficiency and productivity of change by standardizing communication and ensures that all employees communicate in a manner and language understood by all.

8

BENCHMARKING

Allan M. Hoffman
John Holzhüter

"Creativity is not the finding of a thing, but the making something out of it after it is found."

—James Russell Lowell

EDUCATIONAL BENCHMARKING:
ONE SIZE DOES NOT FIT ALL

The term *benchmarking* was first used by cobblers as a way to make a pattern for shoes. A customer would put their foot on the bench, and markings would be made to ensure the proper modification of the shoe template. As industry became both more efficient and more competitive, a modified concept of benchmarking was applied to measure overall quantity and quality standards, as well as the effectiveness of individual worker performance. A standardization of productivity indictors (overall time, cost per product, and percentage of flaws) afforded a common structure of performance comparisons. Initially, it was a tool applied to calculate internal performance levels and then to compare such levels to those of rival companies. The primary focus of business benchmarking was a means of maximizing a competitive edge; copying a successful, competing product; or exploiting a competitor's performance gaps.

In the 1980s, the concept of benchmarking began to blend with aspects of the total quality management (TQM) movement and evolve into a dynamic process that quantified the impact(s) of innovation. This allowed for the ongoing adaptation and continual improvement of a core group of industry need-based targets addressing effectiveness concerns. By the 1990s, applications of benchmarking began to extend past the private sector to public institutional applications. Michael Spendolini, in his 1992 book, defined benchmarking as the "continuous, systematic process for evaluating the products, services, and work processes of organizations that are recognized as representing best practices for the purpose of organizational improvement." By the middle of the decade, it had developed into a widely utilized system for improving the performance of both public sector and governmental organizations from overall output and efficiency standards to individual and departmental performance goals. It provided a base template for improvement and evolution.

As discussed in previous chapters, higher learning tended to be slow in the adoption of any "natural selection" process. Its insular tendencies, deeply rooted in hierarchal preferences, did not easily foster the environment needed for successful benchmarking. In fact, the models entrenched in the higher education system tended to stymie all of the key components needed to support the benchmarking process. Self-assessment, analyses of systemic effectiveness, peer comparison, and opportunities to implement experimental changes were met with fear and resistance. This established additional roadblocks to the process, specifically:

- the goals and objectives proposed by institutional leaders were often not shared by the lower levels of staff,
- there was limited high-level support for mechanisms promoting open and honest dialogue,
- the potential for rapid change was viewed as a threat to institutional effectiveness,
- high levels of "fear of retribution" muted criticism of the status quo,

- information sharing across interdepartmental and hierarchal levels was intermittent and infrequent, and
- there was minimal flexibility to implement changes without upper-level approval.

With federal requirements and employer endorsement of purely objective success models championed by the Reagan administration, the adoption of benchmarking by higher education was inevitable. Independent, external evaluation of international tertiary education success rates had caused near-panic in public and governmental circles. Administrators, facing ever-increasing mandates from federal and state accreditation agencies, recognized that only through numeric illustrations of process improvement could they retain greater levels of institutional control. Of course, benchmarking worked exceedingly well in the academic setting and in unexpected areas, like teacher retention and student satisfaction. By combining it with TQM and quality improvement initiatives, illustrations of national successes became increasingly common.

In 2009, President Obama promulgated the goal that by 2020 the United States will become the top-ranked country in the world for college degrees. In 2008, the United States produced 2.3 million associate's and bachelor's degrees. To become the world leader, U.S. institutions will need to produce an additional 13.3 million degrees. Innovated benchmarking will play a key role in making this dream a reality. Together, all institutions of tertiary education will share best practices and document successes, partnering in ways previously not fathomed.

Institutional communication and joint commitment to this national goal is replacing the overriding competition formerly present in higher education. The following success stories are snapshots of many great things to come.

BENCHMARKING FOR INNOVATION

Scott Epstein

Innovation has achieved a "critical mass" in higher education. *Critical mass* is basically defined as the moment when sufficient interest in a product, service, movement, or trend is achieved that the product, service, movement, or trend becomes the new standard that everyone wishes to acquire or join. Achieving critical mass in any change process usually starts out as a slowly evolving phenomenon; however, there comes a moment when the balance shifts in its favor and changes occur rapidly. That moment is described as the "tipping point" by Malcolm Gladwell is his widely acclaimed book of the same name published in 2000. The tipping point also involves a catalyst—some slight change in the way the product, service, movement, or trend is perceived that causes the "tip." Understanding the catalytic factors are important now for colleges and universities to clearly see the road ahead toward the widespread adoption of quality principles in higher education.

For decades, traditional higher education in America had been able to withstand challenges rather easily. Institutions were internally focused, without a clear understanding of their strengths and weaknesses, reactive in their approach to competitiveness, and poorly informed of students' true requirements. There were feeble efforts to innovate. This has changed with the emergence of quality improvement programs in America's colleges and universities, and such programs have caused benchmarking to grow in scope and focus in higher education. Benchmarking has evolved into a "quick fix" for making quick business performance improvement. Benchmarking is a systematic and scientific methodology for comparing performance between organizations to evaluate the relative excellence of their alternative business practices based on the measured achievements of analytical benchmarks. Benchmarking, however, is not a quick fix; it is a rigorous process that requires learning about one's own processes and coordinating logistics of study mission to other organizations, measurement and analysis of sustained work process performance through the detailed mapping of processes, and head-to-head evaluation of performance differences.

In the development of a quality improvement system, benchmarking has a unique place as both a tool to stimulate improvement and a management technique that aids in strategic positioning of an organization. Ever since Roger Milliken declared in 1990 that "benchmarking is the art of stealing shamelessly," it has grown in scope and focus, leading to many hidden opportunities. More colleges and universities are using benchmarking as a tool to accelerate innovation efforts. The objective is to accelerate the strategic change leading to both breakthrough and continuous improvement in processes, thereby resulting in enhanced student and other stakeholder satisfaction, lower operating costs, and improved competitive advantage by adapting best practices and process improvements of those institutions and external organizations that are recognized for superior performance.

There is a group of institutions that are no longer willing to accept "business as usual" and have successfully escaped the "not invented here" syndrome. The Continuous Quality Improvement Network (CQIN) is a consortium of colleges, universities, nonprofits, and corporate organizations focused on performance excellence in higher education. Every year, CQIN works with a learning partner to develop a summer institute where member organizations benchmark against an enterprise outside of their field. Past learning partners have included the Ritz-Carleton Hotel Company, Motorola University, Saturn Corporation, the Walt Disney Company, Poudre Valley Health Systems, Fortune 100's "Best Places to Work in America" companies (Southwest Airlines, the Container Store), Starbucks Coffee, 3M Corporation, and the Mayo Clinic Healthcare System.

Those who work in higher education have observed good ideas around them and rarely are they adapted to meet their needs and situations. They are exposed to great customer service as a part of their personal lives and rarely adopt these exceptional practices and good ideas to their work environment. Participation in summer institutes brings a good return on investment for students. CQIN summer institutes provide the venue for institutional learning and the opportunity to identify new approaches that blend into an institution's overall quality strategy and can be used for process improvement. Benchmarking with external sources has become an enabler for achieving and maintaining high levels of competitiveness.

CEOs of CQIN schools avoid the syndrome to seek the popular—adopting what is new and worshiping what is popular without making a critical assessment of its validity or applicability. These are weaknesses that are inherent in many "artlike" benchmarking processes. Taking a walk in a manufacturing plant does not constitute a benchmarking site visit—this is industrial tourism. Brief conversations with colleagues at a conference are not benchmarking—these are chats. CQIN summer institutes include three elements: definition of a concept or technique to study, performance measurement of the object, and comparison to other similar objects in order to determine which alternative has achieved the best capability and why.

The effect of CQIN summer institutes is an active dialogue among CQIN schools as well as the sharing of best practices. Some examples of innovation include:

- the translation of the Toyota production system of lean manufacturing to improve course scheduling and financial aid,
- the delivery of exemplary customer service as practiced by the Ritz-Carlton Hotel Company
- the implementation of 3M's Seven Pillars of Innovation—better known as the "Seven Habits of Highly Innovative Corporations," and
- the adaptation of Saturn Corporation's use of self-managed teams to increase the level of employee empowerment.

CQIN summer institutes forces participating institutions to examine their current performance over time against the best practices, competitor performance, and best observed performance over a short time and/or predicted performance based on simulation or modeling. The paradigm of goal setting is changed from the traditional incremental improvement over some baseline to breakthrough improvement levels.

THE NATIONAL COMMUNITY COLLEGE BENCHMARK PROJECT (NCCBP)

Jeff Seybert

The NCCBP measures a wide array of over 120 two-year colleges' input and output indicators encompassing student learning outcomes, access, workforce development, faculty and staff, human resources, and finance variables at the institutional level. This broad scope assists project participants in evaluating and benchmarking faculty load and instructional costs in a broader context.

In 2002–2003, the Community College Benchmark Task Force, a group of institutional research representatives from large prominent community colleges and the League for Innovation in the Community College, responded to the rapidly growing demand for accountability in higher education by designing and implementing an approach to benchmarking community college outcomes. Over the years, the NCCBP has become self-sustaining and grown into the largest national community college data collection/sharing consortium in the United States, with more than 330 participating community colleges since its inception. Among these are the state systems in Colorado, Florida, Hawaii, Indiana (Ivy Tech), Kentucky, New York, Pennsylvania, and Tennessee. In addition, several large community college districts have also participated, including Austin (Texas), Alamo (Texas), Chicago (Illinois), Collin County (Texas), Dallas (Texas), El Paso (Texas), Kansas City (Kansas and Missouri), Maricopa (Arizona), Miami Dade (Florida), Portland (Oregon), and St. Louis (Missouri). In 2010, a record number of more than 270 two-year institutions enrolled.

Methodology   NCCBP data are collected at the institutional level. The data-collection process begins annually in January and ends in July. Until 2010, the principal data-collection instrument was a Microsoft Excel workbook, including definitions of data elements, instructions, and data-entry forms on separate worksheets. Beginning in 2011, all participating institutions began entering their data directly on the new NCCBP website (www.NCCBP.org), which allows automatic calculation of all project benchmarks. This leads to a faster analytic turnaround time, and thus participants receive project reports much earlier in the year. The participant-only sector of the project's website, accessible only with an assigned login and password, provides access to national and in some cases regional aggregate reports, the peer analysis functionality, and the best practices report.

The NCCBP data-collection process checks for missing and inconsistent data automatically. Participating institutions are required to address all data entry errors before they can proceed to the next validation step, the outlier check. At this stage in the data-verification process, institutions' benchmark values are compared with means of values reported by all participants. Participants are then prompted to confirm the accuracy of any "outlier" data (+/- two standard deviations from the mean). Updated benchmark values then become bases for the annual reports.

Project Results   NCCBP subscribers have access to three bench-marking functionalities: (1) national and system aggregate data reports, (2) the peer comparison tool, and (3) the best practices report:

1. The national aggregate reports illustrate percentile ranks of the participating college on each of the 120+ benchmarks. The reports also provide the tenth, twenty-fifth, fiftieth (median), seventy-fifth, and ninetieth percentile for each benchmark in the entire national dataset. Institutions also receive individual system aggregate reports if an intact college system or district has enrolled in the project. Some participating colleges use selected NCCBP benchmarks as key performance indicators (KPIs), which arise from their institution's mission statement and can be used to track institutional progress quantitatively over time.

2. The NCCBP's peer comparison tool lets subscribers select comparable institutions in one of two ways: directly from the list of project participants or on the basis of institutional demographics, such as the size of the unrestricted operating budget, IPEDS enrollment size, minority student population, and others. Participants are then able to select individual benchmarks to compare with those of their peer group. To maintain individual college data confidentiality, this functionality requires the participant to select at least five peer institutions. Individual institutional identities are then masked and the participant can access peer data knowing that the filtered dataset only contains results of the selected peer group.

3. For each NCCBP benchmark, the best practices report identifies all institutions that scored above the eightieth percentile (or in some cases, below the twentieth percentile). The participating institutions can then contact "best practice" colleges to determine the educational programs, initiatives, and innovations that underlie their achievement on a given benchmark.

Uses of NCCBP Data   NCCBP benchmarks have provided the basis for strategic planning and quality improvement efforts at community colleges across the nation. Participants utilize aggregate results and peer comparisons to inform local quality improvement initiatives and accreditation requirements [for example, peer comparison requirements in the NCA Higher Learning Commission's Academic Quality Improvement Program (AQIP)]. NCCBP benchmarks have been incorporated into performance processes, such as the Tennessee Higher Education System performance funding model, and they play an important role as part of strategic planning processes in multicollege systems. Participants use comparative data provided by the NCCBP for institutional program reviews; assessment initiatives; and discussions of such issues as course retention, success rates, and program completions (Juhnke, 2006). Other colleges have incorporated NCCBP benchmarks into their institutional scorecards and executive dashboards to provide a quick performance overview to executives and boards of trustees.

The NCCBP serves as a higher education transparency and accountability instrument that provides community college administrators, faculty, and institutional researchers with the necessary peer comparison tools to effectively pursue targeted quality-improvement processes, prepare accreditation reports, and provide the executive leadership of participating institutions with systematic and regularly provided quantitative indicators, leading the way to enhanced institutional effectiveness. For more information, please visit the website http://www.nccbp.org.

FACULTY DEVELOPMENT

Allan M. Hoffman

"Creative activity could be described as a type of learning process where teacher and pupil are located in the same individual."

—Arthur Koestler

BUILDING ON COMMITMENTS TO INNOVATIVE INTERNAL LEARNING

The threat of competition in the recruitment and retention of good teaching and research staff remains a longstanding reality for administrators. Developing, attracting, and retaining effective faculty, with the sum of human knowledge doubling every five or ten years in some fields, remains a daunting task. Successful institutions have come to recognize that a strong commitment to the development of staff competencies and the fostering of career growth builds both stronger teachers and stronger relationships. While staff development was an integral component for many private businesses starting in the 1950s, for many tertiary schools it was little more than a social afterthought until the mid 1980s. With resurgence in higher education enrollment and many teachers retiring, schools worked to attract new staff from the ranks of business and industry professionals. Many required training to help them convert their practical knowledge into effective teaching methodologies. This short-term need led to the widespread expansion of faculty development programming nationwide.

By the dawn of the 1990s, it had become widely recognized that investing in faculty development was a necessary business practice in an increasingly competitive environment. It was imperative to keep staff informed and up to date, ensure they were connected with industry peers, and bind them to the values and goals of the institution. By the mid 1990s, due to strengthening international economies and global academic competition, there was increasing demand for good faculty from institutions abroad. In 1994, the World Bank issued a paper that noted a "high quality and well motivated teaching staff and a supportive professional culture are essential in building excellence" (*Higher Education*, 1994). The United Nations Educational, Scientific, and Cultural Organization (UNESCO) recognized the important role of higher education staffing when it passed a recommendation on the topic at its general conference in Paris in November 1997. Tertiary institutions recognized that they must develop long-term strategies, not only to retain tenured staff, but also to mentor and develop the educators of the future. Faulty development programs began to expand to include all-staff offerings and to incorporate new technologies into their delivery methods.

By 2008, institutions were incorporating adjunct faculty development and online training offerings into their staff development master plans. Surveys and improvement teams agreed that development programming instilled a sense of individual value and worth. Retention benchmarking studies clearly showed that staff loyalty and recidivism were linked to more than just compensation packages and institutional prestige. Faculty expected to be mentored, to be challenged, and to have continuing educational success recognized as part of their career plans and merit metrics. They anticipated institutional dedication to cutting-edge innovations in staff development would be on par with the focus given to market demands for course offerings.

Today, more than ever, institutions of tertiary education rely on high-caliber staff to buttress institutional reputation and strengthen market share. More than just snacks and games, staff members expect development programming tailored to their individual needs. They request online opportunities that recognize the value of staff time and pre- and post-feedback to give them evaluation opportunities for improving training effectiveness. More than just a "once a quarter focus," faculty demand ongoing and constant commitment to helping them to be more effective in the classroom, more successful in their fields, and more motivated in their career aspirations. The following success stories highlight developmental programming that develops and values the faculty it is designed to serve.

EMPLOYEE SUCCESS AT WESTERN TECHNICAL COLLEGE

Lee Rasch

Have you ever experienced the anxiety associated with the performance-review process? Did you feel that the process seemed to focus on areas for improvement and not on the good work produced? Did you feel the performance-rating system was arbitrary and did not reflect excellence in performance? The employee success policy at Western Technical College is an approach to human resource development that emphasizes the inherent ability of every employee to grow and succeed. Developed in 1995, the policy drew upon the theories of W. Edwards Deming and others, who contend that the overwhelming majority of all employees provide a positive addition to the workplace. These employees best benefit from a plan to help them grow professionally and personally. Subsequent research by the Gallup Organization reinforces this, emphasizing the importance of building upon employee strengths. The employee success policy is an alternative to the traditional performance appraisal, which frequently focuses on shortcomings and improvement areas.

To be certain, performance problems occur. The employees who struggle in performance are better served through a concentrated effort focusing on specific activities designed to help them redirect their performance in a positive manner. In all cases, the key is the firm belief by the supervisor that the employee can indeed grow and succeed. There are three components to the employee success policy: the employee success plan, the probationary performance appraisal, and the special performance appraisal. The essential element is the employee success plan. Each employee is encouraged to develop a plan for professional and personal growth and improvement. This plan is shared in a confidential dialog with the immediate supervisor with the goal of mutually developing an action plan for achieving growth. Aggregated information is compiled in the human resource office to assist the college in planning for professional development opportunities. The employee success plan is designed to be positive in nature. Supervisors are encouraged to build upon employee strengths. Furthermore, the employee success plan is recognized to be a living document, with ongoing changes and developments. Because of this, the dialog sessions between employee and supervisor are intended to be ongoing and frequent.

The second component is the probationary performance appraisal. Western Technical College does not embrace the concept of the traditional performance appraisal. Nonetheless, the college recognizes that new employees may on occasion struggle in adapting to the work environment. For example, new instructors may have substantial experience in their field of work, yet they may lack the formal experience or preparation in teaching. In some cases, this may lead to poor performance in the classroom. As a result, the college interprets the probationary period to be a continuation of the hiring process. Once the new employee has successfully completed the probationary period, the employee no longer undergoes an annual performance appraisal. The employee success plan serves as the guiding and development framework for all nonprobationary employees.

The final component is the special performance appraisal. The college embraces the 95/5 rule as proposed by W. Edwards Deming. Essentially, the philosophy suggests that 95 percent of all employees are conscientious and productive. However, at any given time, 5 percent of the employee group struggles in performance. There can be many reasons for this poor performance. The employee success policy does not suggest that these "5-percenters" are bad employees. Indeed, it is recognized that there can be many factors that could lead to poor performance (stress, burnout, family problems, and physical ailments, to name a few). However, the college must initially focus on work performance in attempting to address the issues with these employees.

The special performance appraisal is developed with the immediate supervisor and offers specific directions and a timeline (generally six months to one year) for improvement. It also includes specific consequences if poor performance continues. In order for this process to succeed, it is necessary for the supervisor to ensure that several key elements are present. First, the supervisor must be very specific in developing positive goal statements and consequences for poor performance. Second, there must be periodic reviews of performance (monthly in some cases). Finally, and most important, the supervisor must be able to convey to the employee that there is support for success. This is a crucial element. If the employee believes that the supervisor is "out to get them," positive results cannot be expected from their performance plan. At the same time, this does not suggest that the consequences for continued poor performance are not real. The power in the special performance appraisal exists in the combined message of support from the supervisor coupled with very real consequences for noncompliance with meeting agreed improvement goals. Once the employee has successfully completed the special performance appraisal, he or she returns to the use of the employee success plan as the tool for growth and improvement.

While there are many factors that may contribute to a positive work environment, the longstanding use of the employee success policy is considered a key factor in helping Western Technical College maintain an organizational climate that is above the national norm (Cerbo and Mercer, 2009).

ACADEMY FOR TEACHING EXCELLENCE
FOR FACULTY DEVELOPMENT

Gina Schochenmaier, Jeff Rabey, and Jeff Bonsall

As with many other community colleges, Iowa Western has been exploring ways to help provide meaningful, financially responsible faculty development. In addition to the needs of the full-time faculty, the college was looking for ways to better engage its part-time faculty. The Academy for Teaching Excellence provides an in-house development experience for full-time and part-time faculty. Held three times yearly, the academy is a series of Saturday mini-conferences, which all faculty are invited to attend. A keynote speaker, along with several breakout sessions, are offered with each academy. Full-time faculty are required to attend one per year, while part-time faculty are encouraged to attend at least one per year. The focus of the day is teaching and learning. Mini-session presenters are generally faculty members who share their best practices. The organizers are committed to keeping the content focused on faculty needs in the classroom. Administrative tasks and presentations heavily dependent on research with few practical applications are discouraged.

Previous to having the academy, the college tried to hold workshops for faculty throughout the academic year, scheduling the sessions during the daytime hours when faculty could present the sessions. Unfortunately, most of the adjunct instructors were never able to attend, and many full-time faculty could not take advantage of the sessions because of their teaching schedules. Attendance at these initial sessions sometimes numbered only two to four people.

A group of academic administrators discussed how to improve what the college was doing for faculty development. The goals were multifold:

1. improve teaching and learning for students;
2. bring faculty together to share best practices;
3. offer a venue for faculty to present professionally;
4. provide networking opportunities, especially for adjunct instructors; and
5. serve as a regional source for faculty development.

Once the goals were identified, discussions evolved as to how to best meet these goals. The template for the Academy for Teaching Excellence began to take form. The day's format was to mimic large, national conferences yet on a smaller scale.

The first academy was held in August 2007. It was extremely well received by the participants. It took approximately eight weeks to develop the format and agenda for the first event. The initial cost was under $2,000. That cost has increased as the number of participants has risen (both breakfast and lunch are included) as well as the costs for a keynote presenter. There are three full-time college employees who help to organize and present the academy. The college provides meeting rooms, food, printing, and publicity. Initially, the academy was promoted as a faculty development opportunity for adjunct faculty. As the academy became more popular, the college began to move toward making attendance at one of the academies mandatory for full-time faculty. This met with some resistance from a handful of very vocal faculty. Eventually one faculty contract day was exchanged for one academy day. Almost all of the faculty agree the event is very worthwhile but would prefer it was offered during the week. However, if the academy was moved to a weekday, very few of our adjuncts and high school (dual enrollment) instructors would be able to attend. It is not economically feasible to offer two separate events.

Another obstacle was that of funding, as our general college budget was cut last year substantially. We have trimmed down printing costs, examined food costs, and tried to market the event to outside groups with the goal of bringing in revenue from the academy. Costs are directly tied to the number of attendees. An academy can range from $2,000 to $10,000, depending on food costs and keynote speaker fees. For this expense, however, there are 40 to 150 faculty members receiving information that helps them improve teaching at the college. If we were to send everyone away for a one-day meeting at a cost of $100, that would total $4,000 to $15,000. The academy is a very fiscally efficient form of faculty development for the college.

At the end of each Academy for Teaching Excellence, participants complete a survey. The organizers of the event respond to their suggestions. Each academy addresses specific needs identified by the faculty through the surveys. The attendance is also monitored closely. Increased attendance can be an indicator that that academy is perceived as relevant and valuable.

Currently we publish all the presentations for the Academy for Teaching Excellence electronically but do not yet have them available on a public website. Development is underway to have a Web presence within the next year.

FACULTY CERTIFICATION AND MENTORSHIP AT THE UNIVERSITY OF PHOENIX

Adam Honea and Barbara Taylor

The University of Phoenix requires faculty candidates to participate in a faculty certification and mentorship process. Administrators of the faculty believe this training is crucial to the quality of the university's online teaching. A majority of the faculty members are experienced practitioners who work in their professions and teach part time. Faculty candidates are first screened on academic credentials and work experience. If the candidate has either a master's or a doctorate degree and appropriate work experience, he or she is then invited to participate in the University of Phoenix faculty certification and mentorship process.

The faculty certification process presents both pedagogy and best practices. Faculty candidates are introduced to the university's teaching/learning model and are provided training in specific skills, such as classroom management and assessing student learning. The teaching/learning model focuses on active learning, collaboration, and application of relevant constructs through facilitation. Because many of the candidates are practitioners, they may have no prior experience or training in teaching skills.

The certification process is an intensive four-week training process administered as two modules: core certification and specialization certification. All faculty candidates complete the core module. After successfully completing the core module, faculty candidates complete the appropriate specialization module based on the college in which the faculty candidate is to facilitate. The online faculty certification is conducted in an online classroom and is structured to model a typical University of Phoenix class. The candidate completes assignments and participates in discussions, as do online students. Candidates are assessed weekly by certification trainers and provide suggestions for improvement using a standardized evaluation form.

When a candidate successfully completes certification, they are ready for mentorship. In the mentorship, the candidate works with a faculty mentor before, during, and after the candidate instructs his or her first class. The mentor evaluates candidates weekly during the mentorship class using a standardized evaluation form. Candidates are provided suggestions for improvement. At the end of the mentorship class, the mentor makes a recommendation on the preparedness of the faculty candidate to join the faculty of the University of Phoenix.

The University of Phoenix has focused on providing working adults access to higher education. Experience demonstrates that working adults benefit from relevant coursework that is taught by academically

FACULTY DEVELOPMENT   103

qualified faculty members who are experienced practitioners. A possible downside to using practitioner faculty members is they may not have extensive teaching experience. The University of Phoenix uses the faculty certification and mentorship process to ensure a base level of quality in teaching in all courses.

The University of Phoenix has always used mentorships; the current faculty certification and mentorship process evolved out of the original mentorship process and thus does not have a specific timeline for development and implementation. There has not been resistance within the organization to the faculty orientation and mentorship process. The resistance has mostly come from faculty candidates who have experience teaching at other institutions and do not believe they should have to go through the process. The University of Phoenix simply requires all new faculty candidates to go through the process. The faculty certification and mentorship process utilizes the key components of in-process measurement and feedback points consisting of weekly and final certification trainer reports, weekly and final mentor reports, and student end-of-course surveys in the mentorship course. Student end-of-course surveys and periodic faculty evaluations constitute post–faculty certification and mentorship process measurement.

⑩

STUDENT RETENTION

Allan M. Hoffman
John Holzhüter

"There's a way to do it better—find it."

—Thomas Edison

RETAINING STUDENTS THROUGH TARGETED SUPPORT AND SOCIAL ENRICHMENT

While the overall duration of student attendance, total costs of completion, postgraduate employment rate, and percentage of students defaulting on their student loans are important metrics in assessing academic effectiveness, student retention figures trump all. High retention levels ensure cash flow through tuition revenues; increase the odds of state, federal, and private grant-based support; and produce a supportive parent and alumni base. There are a myriad of reasons that students choose to leave college prior to graduation, and the impacting factors are highly personal and individualized. Theoretical models can accurately predict the impact of common factors, including the specific trending of minority, first-generation and nontraditional group status. It is also possible to identify commonalities that appear to relate to general, underlying causes. These include student self-efficacy and locus of control, kyri-archal beliefs, background variables, academic and organizational factors, and social and environmental factors. A student's perception and interpretation of these factors can impact the odds of successful degree completion.

Regardless of the predictive model, it is clear that, while academic preparedness and abilities are important, the attitudes a student forms about the institution and feelings of value, support, and validation instilled by faculty and administration significantly impact the decision to stay enrolled. Increasingly there is a growing awareness that new students need more than general financial aid assistance, freshman orientation, and subject tutors. Combining internal institutional data assessment with familiarity of the psychological and sociopsychological theories surrounding student retention, institutions have developed innovative programming approaches to motivate students to stay in school. These include outreach partnerships with high schools to develop academic skills, bridging programs that offer concordance classes to high school seniors, programming for parents and guardians, student support services that target coping methodologies and barrier reduction strategies, social programming, sensitivity training for staff and students, and the incorporation of exit interview results into ongoing process improvement initiatives.

Innovative retention programming models are now tailoring student mentoring and individualized goal setting to fit the targeted social needs of specific students. Efforts combining academic support with role-model sponsorship and immersion in a variety of art, cultural, and cocurricular events are becoming more popular and showing great success. Additionally, students are being encouraged to forge connections beyond the campus through community service opportunities and faith-based experiences. Clearly, because institutions are successfully meeting the full array of developmental and academic needs students bring with them to their educational experience, students are motivated to stay engaged and enrolled. The following success stories highlight unique approaches to the pernicious struggle of ensuring that students return to school until they graduate.

MEETING THE NEEDS OF UNDERSERVED STUDENTS

Daniel Lowery, Eugene Finnegan, Darren Henderson, Dionne Jones-Malone, and Joseph Kovach

Calumet College of St. Joseph is located in northwestern Indiana and serves the urban communities of Hammond, Gary, and East Chicago, as well as the southeast side of Chicago. Although the college now offers degree-completion programs for professionals and four graduate programs, our sponsoring religious order founded the college more than fifty years ago to provide educational opportunities for an underserved urban population. The college has remained true to this mission. We are routinely recognized as one of the most diverse four-year institutions of higher learning in the Midwest.

Serving this particular population has proven challenging, however. A significant number of our students are drawn from among the poorest-performing K–12 schools in the state. Most are first-generation college attendees. Many work and have family responsibilities. And these challenges have become more widespread and acute among our student body.

Given this, faculty and key administrative staff members launched a comprehensive three-year initiative at the beginning of the 2006–2007 academic year. Our research-based Centering on Retention and Enrollment, or CORE, Initiative was designed to ensure that we don't just churn underprepared students. We were motivated to pursue this effort by our mission but also by a renewed appreciation for the competitive environment in which we find ourselves. Our key competitors recently raised their admission standards. We were better positioned, as a result, to serve as a four-year alternative to the state's community college system. Our mission, our competitors strategic repositioning, and our long and successful history of serving underprepared and first-generation students thus pointed to the same strategic objective: the achievement of excellence in providing undergraduate educational programs for underserved students.

We recognized that we would need to do more in order to remain true to our mission and to achieve our goals. To this end, the CORE Initiative was developed during the 2006–2007 academic year. In the following year, we processed its various components through our faculty, administrative, and board decision-making processes. The initiative's several components were then implemented during the 2008–2009 academic year. They include:

- the prescribed sequencing of our general education curriculum in order to ensure that students are provided with opportunities early in their college careers to develop the foundational knowledge, skills, abilities, and personal dispositions needed to succeed;
- a for-credit, weeklong orientation course designed to help us connect more quickly with students and better prepare them for success in the classroom;
- the adoption of linked courses delivered to cohorts of freshman who participate in learning communities; the administration of a robust set of assessment tools in our orientation and general education capstone courses (Collegiate Assessment of Academic Proficiency [CAAP], Beginning College Survey of Student Engagement [BCSSE], learning styles, and career orientation);
- the assignment of staff mentors who communicate regularly with students through their first year with us; and
- the development of student portfolios, which include transcripts, early alerts, and assessment test scores, as a foundation for discussions involving mentors and mentees.

None of these components is original per se. They are, however, packaged in a way that is quite innovative. They fully reflect key findings in the literature pertaining to underprepared students. The mix of strategies is consistent with our mission. The several components build on our strengths. And they are fully responsive to the competitive environment in which the college finds itself. Together, these several strategies provide for a freshman experience that is quite different from the experience students have at most other institutions of higher learning.

The chief barrier in developing a comprehensive program of this kind was conceptual in nature and pertained to the traditional roles of faculty and staff. Early on, key faculty members recognized that the image of the faculty member as a sole practitioner who is in total control of his or her courses and the pedagogical methods employed needed to give way to a more student-centered model. This does not mean that faculty members must surrender their autonomy; they need, however, to exercise their autonomy in collaboration with others, not as faculty members per se but as a faculty, a community of scholars as dedicated to learning as it is to teaching. Additionally, we recognized that our faculty would need to work in closer collaboration with professional staff who serve students as advisors, coaches, and tutors. We were fortunate to have senior faculty members who embraced this understanding of the academic calling.

We were greatly aided in this effort in two distinct ways. First, the Lilly Endowment awarded the college a grant in the amount of $375,000 in support of the initiative. The funds have been used to hire faculty and support staff and to underwrite an expanded array of assessment activities. Second, Calumet College of St. Joseph participates in AQIP, the Academic Quality Improvement Program, an accreditation methodology that encourages institutions of higher learning to focus on quality improvement and a select set of projects for which they choose to be held accountable to the Higher Learning Commission. The orientation program and learning community components of our CORE Initiative were developed as AQIP projects.

The CORE Initiative has now been implemented for two full years. In our first year, we saw modest but encouraging improvement in our retention numbers and in the number of students who stay on track toward their goals. The posttest portion of our package of assessment instruments were scheduled to be administered for the first time in the fall 2010 semester. Further, key components of the initiative were tweaked after the 2008–2009 academic year and again after the 2009–2010 academic year. Most notably, the content of the general education curriculum was updated and made more rigorous. We are in this effort for the long haul and are confident that students are better served at Calumet College of St. Joseph as a result. Additional information about the CORE Initiative can be obtained by contacting Daniel Lowery, Ph.D., vice president for academic affairs at Calumet College of St. Joseph, 2400 New York Avenue, Whiting, IN 46394, or at dlowery@ccsj.edu.

SPRINGBOARD TO SUCCESS—FULL-SERVICE ORIENTATION FOR NEW FRESHMEN

David Sill

As part of an AQIP action project titled Reshape New Student Transition, Southern Illinois University–Edwardsville (SIUE) developed a new freshman orientation and registration program that has continued since 2004. Prior to 2004, an optional half-day program called Pre-Entry Advising and Registration (PEAR) focused only on advisement, testing, and registration. The new program, Springboard to Success, which replaced PEAR, was required of all new freshmen, not optional, and started out in two versions, as a full-day or two-day program. In 2008, the one-day option was dropped, and Springboard became an overnight, residential program.

Springboard to Success welcomes new students to the university community and provides academic and student life information. It advises and enrolls students for the fall semester, lets students know the student learning objectives, and gives new freshmen opportunities to get to know other students. Admitted new freshmen sign up online for Springboard to Success. On the first day, the new freshmen participate in welcoming, informational, and recreational sessions. They have meals in small groups with Springboard student leaders. After spending the night in the residence hall, students complete registration, meet with advisors, and enroll in courses. Parallel to but separate from the new freshman program is a parent and family program. The two programs come together during the advisement sessions on the second day.

The project achieved three major improvements. First, by requiring the program for all new freshmen, it reduced and almost eliminated ad hoc advising and enrollment for new freshmen. Second, it included orientation for both students and families in preparation for a successful freshman year. Third, the schedule completed registration and enrollment by the first week of July, eliminating crisis management for scheduling freshman-level courses at the beginning of the fall semester.

With the opening of our first residence hall in 1994, SIUE began changing from a commuter to a residential campus, significantly increasing the traditional student population. By 2002, we had completed two more residence halls so that 1,500 students lived on campus in residence halls, and the majority of new freshmen started as residential students. In fewer than ten years, we went from no residential new freshmen to more than one thousand residential new freshmen. At the same time, we retained our commitment to serving commuting and nontraditional students. The AQIP leadership team in the provost office developed the action project Reshape New Student Transition to help us respond to challenges that these different student populations presented. Second-year persistence averaged 69.5 percent between 1990 and 2000, with only 63 percent in 1993. We wanted to improve that persistence rate. At the same time, the significant new residential student population presented us with challenges for orientation, student life, and maturity that we had not confronted before.

It took approximately two years to develop and implement Springboard to Success. The program was piloted in 2003 while we studied the existing orientation and registration programs. When developing the proposal and planning for Springboard to Success, the piloted program became the model. We fully implemented Springboard for the fall 2004 entering freshman class.

The original cost was $155,000, with fee revenue covering $131,000 of this cost. For startup, we hired a half-time secretary and assigned responsibility to an admissions counselor for organizing and implementing the program. Indirect development costs included time for the ten-member working group of faculty, staff, and administrators that designed and planned implementation.

We faced two types of resistance. First, because SIUE began as a commuter institution, a number of faculty, staff, and administrators resisted requiring an overnight, two-day program. Resistance to an overnight program was overcome by making the two-day version optional, allowing time to show that the overnight program could work for our students. The working group created two options, a one-day program for commuting students and an overnight program for residential students. The original proposal scheduled sessions to accommodate a projected one thousand students in one-day sessions and six hundred students in overnight programs. Once the mechanics were worked out and we demonstrated a history of success, the resistance evaporated. The program now is a two-day program only. Second, we faced resistance to the startup costs included in the first proposal. To overcome this resistance, we reduced the $67,000 initial subsidy to $24,000 by modifying the plan.

The program is supported by fees, currently $150 for each participating student and $25 for each participating family member, which brings in more than $200,000 each year. Other costs are the normal operating costs for advising and enrolling new students that we would have even without this program. Savings include a better course-staffing pattern and better class scheduling because there is no need for adding new class sections a week before classes start.

We created the program to increase the number of new freshmen participating in orientation and to register and enroll new freshmen early enough to facilitate course scheduling. Accordingly, the first measure of success is participation. Springboard to Success was fully implemented for fall semester 2004. Twenty-one one-day programs were offered from March 30 through May 20, and six overnight programs were offered between June 2 and July 1. Between the day and the overnight programs, 1,626 of the 1,682 new freshmen (96.7 percent) participated in Springboard to Success. For the day program, 995 students (59.2 percent) and 1,152 parents/guests attended; an additional 631 students (37.5 percent) and 588 parents/guests attended the overnight programs.

Information about Springboard to Success is available on the Web, including the agenda, dates, and a copy of the brochure, with a description of the program and a rationale for participation (http://www. siue.edu/prospectivestudents/admitted/springboard.shtml). We have institutionalized the innovation with over 95 percent of new freshmen participating each year. Information about Springboard to Success is included in recruiting and admissions materials. The catalog lists the attendance requirement and a brief description. There will always be some students who cannot participate, and admissions counselors and advisors individually handle the few students who cannot participate.

AN INNOVATIVE MARRIAGE OF ACCOUNTABILITY AND ASSESSMENT FOR IMPROVING THE BEGINNING COLLEGE EXPERIENCE

John N. Gardner and Betsy O. Barefoot

Some educational historians argue that in many ways American colleges and universities are resistant to innovation—that much about higher education is essentially the same as it was in the seventeenth and eighteenth centuries. While it is true that some elements of the academic experience are more or less static, significant educational innovations have improved campus environments and generated greater levels of student learning, satisfaction, and persistence. One such innovation was the process of regional accreditation, which we would posit is the most influential driver today of innovation linked to efforts at quality improvement in the academy. But another innovation, which is the subject of this article, is a model and process developed in 2003 to help institutions evaluate and improve the first year of college for both first-time-in-college and transfer students.

This model, Foundations of Excellence in the First College Year (FoE), administered by the John N. Gardner Institute, resulted from the work of a core group of institute staff and external higher education experts with support from philanthropies, accreditors, and institutions. The intellectual centerpiece of this first-year innovation is a model composed of nine standards of excellence for the first year, termed Foundational Dimensions. But FoE also includes a structured process that enables colleges and universities to engage in an intensive, year-long study of the first year and the development of an evidence-based plan for improvement.

Rationale for the FoE Approach   FoE provides colleges the opportunity to close the gap between good intentions and harsh reality. While the great society certainly provided access to higher education beginning in the late 1960s, legal access to higher education was only a first step. Changes in the law did not guarantee success for the millions of educationally and financially disadvantaged students who suddenly found it possible to go to college. Institutions themselves were often unprepared for these "new students," and consequently high percentages of students did not perform well academically, persist, or graduate. Over the past forty years, the most common reaction to student underperformance has been the creation of interventions in the form of piecemeal "programs." But programs, while necessary, are not sufficient to realize real improvement in rates of student progress. FoE provides the missing piece: creation of an overarching evidence-based plan that considers all aspects of the new-student experience—pre-enrollment communication, classroom experiences, out-of-class activities, and relevant policies—and uses evidence to determine the types of programs, practices, and policies that make the greatest positive difference for new students. This plan uses as its foundation the nine aspirational standards of excellence and encourages each institution to carefully evaluate its performance vis-à-vis these standards.

The Gardner Institute's motivations for the development of this process were several. We wanted to:

- increase institutional accountability for student learning and success;
- develop a set of aspirational standards to measure and encourage the pursuit of excellence in the first year;
- move the "student success" conversation beyond retention, which is a minimum standard, to focus instead on the basic question: How could an institution, regardless of its type or level of student readiness, achieve first-year excellence?
- help campuses develop and implement an evidence-based, coherent plan for student success; and
- create partnerships with regional accreditors whereby institutions could be doubly rewarded by linking efforts to improve first-year performance and achieve reaffirmation of accreditation.

As of 2010, FoE's self-study process has been undertaken by 167 colleges and universities. While the pilot testing of FoE was supported by funding from the Atlantic Philanthropies and Lumina Foundation for Education, ongoing costs of participating in FoE are borne solely by institutional participants.

How FoE Uses Assessment   There are multiple forms of assessment within the FoE process:

1. Each campus evaluates its own level of adherence to the nine foundational dimensions. While institute staff members do not perform this evaluation, they provide guidance and direction for the campus's assessment efforts.
2. Some institutions have combined the FoE process with reaffirmation of accreditation, most notably in the Higher Learning Commission, the largest of the six regional accreditors. In such instances the accreditor also serves as an external quality assessor.
3. The institute routinely evaluates its own performance by contracting with external evaluators. To date we have commissioned two external studies of the impact of FoE. The first was a study of the perceived value of the FoE study and planning process, and the second, a specific analysis of retention rates as a function of partici-

pation in FoE. The retention analysis has proved particularly encouraging. Results of an in-house survey of 130 FoE participants from 2003 through 2008 were linked with IPEDS (Integrated Post-secondary Education Data Systems) data. Campuses that reported implementing their FoE action plans to a "high degree" experienced a 5.6 point increase in retention over four years. This represents an overall 8.2 percent average retention rate increase. In the current climate of increased accountability and financial difficulty, such increased retention rates are very compelling indeed.

Transfer Adaptation   Based on the success of the FoE process as originally designed (to develop a comprehensive design for the first year), the process was adapted in 2009–2010 to become the new FoE Transfer Focus. In that year, six public universities participated in the pilot test. In 2010–2011, the institute will conduct a comparable pilot test of an FoE process designed for two-year colleges that want to focus on their service to transfer-bound students. Because student transfer is now the norm in American higher education, the prospects for success and increased demand for FoE Transfer Focus also appear strong. In truth, President Obama's lofty goals for increasing U.S. graduation rates cannot be achieved without developing campus-specific action plans to improve levels of transfer student success.

The institute recruits new cohorts of two- and four-year institutions each year, launching the new work in the summer just before the fall term begins. The FoE process is an example of an educational innovation that has already provided support for a critical mass of public and private two- and four-year institutions and the students whom they serve.

For additional information about the Gardner Institute and the FoE process, go to the institute's websites: www.fyfoundations.org and www.jngi.org.

11

CURRICULUM DEVELOPMENT

Allan M. Hoffman

"The achievement of excellence can only occur if the organization promotes a culture of creative dissatisfaction."

—Lawrence Miller

ASSURING CURRICULA OUTPACES STAKEHOLDER EXPECTATIONS

The dawn of the 1980s ushered in especially difficult times for higher learning in the United States. College entrance requirements had been softened and course prerequisites reduced in an attempt to bolster enrollment. Undergraduate curriculum had become fragmented and too situationally based. Designed to appeal to multiple learning styles (intellectual, visual, aural, and kinesthetic), what emerged was a disjointed course flow that failed to clarify key learning points. Students became confused and dropped out, often after their first year. In addition to declining enrollments, there was an increase in federal scrutiny and mounting public demands for tangible proof of the "value" of a higher education. Tertiary institutions struggled to balance the varied perspectives of diverse stakeholders. Business leaders anticipated the majority of goals for student learning would be driven by end-user demand. State and federal agencies called for systemwide content expectations and uniformity in lesson sequence and evaluation. There was a growing public interest to attach "verifiable mastery" stipulations to all types of subsidized educational funding.

Dwindling cash flows forced cost containment and cost reduction strategies while a barrage of new regulations threatened to strip schools of their accreditation by requiring adherence to standardized and objective-operational metrics. Some long-established schools were forced to close, being too insular or too brittle to survive the onslaught of shifting requirements and straining operation budgets. Other institutions survived this same maelstrom, thriving in these chaotic times by forging new partnerships, harnessing new research and technologies, and shifting emphasis from academic methodologies to better comprehending student learning. Administrators worked to foster an institutionwide understanding of overarching goals by encouraging staff communication and process improvement suggestions. Teachers worked to create a climate of constancy and repetition that reinforced and strengthened student learning.

What emerged was a variety of collaborative and cooperative learning approaches that transcended long-accepted models and afforded more learner control and investment. By the 1990s, learning evaluation methods had been expanded and improved. Critical thinking skill illustrations were valued as much as rote retention, and hands-on and real-world assessments had become popular with educators and stakeholders alike. Educators were encouraged to correlate instructional objectives with changes in observable student behaviors and to propose new ways to maximize learning efficiencies. By incorporating advancements in technology, forming academic consortiums, and exploiting demands for cross-cultural and global competency standards, they were able to introduce thematic and problem-solving protocols across multiple disciplines. Additionally, a myriad of support services and social remediation efforts were mandated to develop both better study habits and healthier coping mechanisms. Tertiary institutions partnered with high schools to better prepare incoming freshman and worked to understand and incorporate employment-sector values and expectations.

Today, pre- and posttesting scores and feedback from student and staff are combined with standardized assessment and licensure scores to assure a complete picture of student learning and retention. This is utilized not only to calibrate programming and illustrate its effectiveness but also to propose enhancements and ensure the continuous improvement of course offerings and majors. Teaching methodologies in basic core areas of emphasis (science, mathematics, computing) integrate experiential learning through labs, fieldtrips, and corporate partnerships. New programming is constantly being developed to keep pace with the needs of the business sector. Students are learning more than just subject theory; they are experiencing practical applications that lead to vocational contemplation, career aspirations, and social engagement. The following success stories exemplify the scope and creativity of innovations in curricula.

NEW PROGRAM DEVELOPMENT—MAINTAINING A TRADITION OF INNOVATION IN HARD TIMES

Patricia A. Breen

The Chicago School of Professional Psychology (TCSPP) has been driven by an innovative spirit since its founding in 1979. Its growth from a single-program graduate institution with fewer than 200 students in 2000 to an education system now serving more than 3,500 students with multiple disciplines, multiple campus locations, and diverse delivery modes reflects its steadfast commitment to avoid steadfastness, that is, to innovate. Its mission documents make this most clear. Its vision is built upon innovation and quality. Its mission is fulfilled through the integration of innovation with theory and practice. And, as articulated as one of its core institutional values, innovation, together with community, service, and education, is essential to TCSPP's identity within an approach to higher education.

The Chicago School (TCS) Education System was created by TCSPP as a means to both preserve the mission and identity of TCSPP and to provide the same academic and business model to support similar innovative and discipline-focused institutions. The mission and vision of TCS Education System deeply reflects its origins in TCSPP: *TCS Education*

System prepares innovative, engaged, purposeful agents of change who serve our global community. TCS Education System is therefore the consortial structure that supports TCSPP, Pacific Oaks College, Santa Barbara Graduate Institute, and the Santa Barbara/Ventura Colleges of Law with various infrastructure services, including market research and project management for new program development. TCS Education System has developed an approach to make better decisions about new programs and to ensure that they have a better chance for success with a well-supported startup.

This approach combines good practices in new product development from the business sector with the practical realities of higher education: a need for mission fit; sustainability; academic quality; and a disciplined, comprehensive implementation plan. TCS Education System's "stage gate" process takes each phase of a new program concept through several points of decision making. Each is meant to build commitment to the concept by progressively ensuring fulfillment of the overarching criteria for approval. These criteria include the potential to meet the institution's strategic growth plan; to meet its mission and academic model; to achieve standards of academic excellence; and to be sustained through enrollment demand, resource stewardship, and competitive positioning.

The process itself is overseen by a New Program Development Committee consisting of the vice presidents of academic planning and development, marketing, admissions, and finance. With the support of market research data and professional project management, the first discovery stage develops the program idea initiated by a "program champion," a faculty member or other member of the community, through to a fuller program concept. These concepts are submitted to a broad representation of multidisciplinary and functional experts from academic affairs, admissions, marketing, finance, information technology, applied professional practice, career services, and others. This group of experts establishes the first gate of the process; the "viability gate." It is their collective opinion regarding their perceptions of practicality and potential as well as fulfillment of the key criteria that allows a concept to pass through this gate and proceed to the next phase. With the New Program Development Committee acting in an advisory capacity, it is the institution's president who makes this decision.

Successful completion of the viability gate furthers the concept through to development of a full program proposal. In this stage the program champion is supported by an external advisory board of subject matter experts in the field to develop the full curriculum outline and assessment infrastructure. The project manger facilitates all of the operational components of the proposal, including the admissions projections, financial pro forma, and related accreditation requirements. At this proposal gate, the full proposal is evaluated by the New Program Development Committee in relation to the four overarching criteria, and recommendations are again presented to the institute president for a decision regarding next steps. The president considers any internal faculty or board recommendations as well.

With successful completion of the proposal gate, the process moves into the development stage in which all support departments, including admissions, marketing, registrar, student affairs, and academic planning and development, prepare for the launch of the program. This work is supported by a comprehensive and coordinated implementation plan of essential tasks, deadlines, interdependencies, and final approvals necessary for launch. This preparation is monitored and approved by the New Program Development Committee at the last decision point: the launch gate. The launch stage results in new students enrolled in the new, mission-driven, sustainable, and academically excellent program.

A crucial driver of its commitment to innovation is curricular. From its origins, TCSPP embraced currency and relevance of the needs of the community as defining its educational program. Among the first of the professional psychology schools to adopt the new "scientist-practitioner" model of education, the school sought to provide future psychologists with the knowledge, skills, and aptitudes required for clinical practice rather than the traditional model rooted more deeply in academic research. Even today, the school continues its quest to lead curricular innovation through its own, recently articulated model: the "engaged practitioner," which evolved through its inclusion of diversity and multicultural awareness as institutional learning goals and therefore community engagement as part of the teaching and learning process.

In addition to TCSPP's educational approaches, much of its growth in the last ten years, in fact, has been due to new and innovative programming in such fields as business psychology, international psychology, forensic psychology, clinical counseling, and applied behavior analysis. Until 2009, TCSPP followed a fairly traditional process for new program development; ideas were generally initiated and developed by the faculty with approvals from the cabinet and board at the appropriate benchmarks. The small and self-contained nature of TCSPP's single campus allowed for well-managed though casual communication and implementation.

Recently, however, internal as well as external changes have challenged the efficacy of this traditional process. Internally, these include the need for objective criteria that reflected the goals of the institution as well as those of an individual campus or department. Sound assessment processes now require a curricular infrastructure based upon a clear and coherent map of outcomes, courses, and program competencies and therefore access to curriculum development specialists. New delivery modes, particularly online, also require access to an instructional designer expert in those modes. TCSPP's own expansion to a multicampus structure and its affiliation with three new colleges, all with new program development goals, created a significantly greater need for institutionwide coordination, communication, and support for implementation as well as a reliable development process itself. Externally, pressures due to increased competition from the for-profit sector and "speed to market" considerations, the increasing complexity of regulatory requirements, and the pace of change in the higher education environment have all increased the risks associated with new programming. Both of these types of pressures have, in turn, increased the need for careful, informed decision making and efficient development and implementation. TCSPP's growth and commitment to innovative, relevant, and current curricula, as well as the growth and commitment of Pacific Oaks College, Santa Barbara Graduate Institute, and Santa Barbara/Ventura Colleges of Law, depend upon an efficient, viable, and disciplined process that seeks to ensure alignment with the institutional mission and strategic plan, which is well designed academically and referenced to curricular standards in the field and which provides data on student and employer market potential in the field.

A group of twenty representing faculty and staff from TCSPP and TCS Education System met in November 2009 to develop the "must haves" for new program development, which reflected both campus and institutional priorities. The group brainstormed the goals and an approach that was then assigned to a smaller task force representing expertise in new program development, market research, online-blended programs, and project management. Their initial concept was presented to the president's cabinet in March 2010 and was continuously refined with input from multiple academic and process experts through to its presentation to the Academic Affairs Committee of the board of trustees in September 2010. Ten new programs are currently in process.

Very little resistance to this process was experienced during its development and implementation. Explicit clarification was regularly needed regarding the fact that the institution (TCSPP, Pacific Oaks College, Santa Barbara Graduate Institute, or the Colleges of Law) was responsible for all decisions regarding a new program adoption and launch and that the role of the TCS Education System New Program Development Committee was facilitative and advisory only.

Dedicated costs for the initial brainstorming meeting, the task force, and the continuous improvement of the process were approximately $39,000. These costs include primarily allocated personnel. The incremental cost of developing a new program, including compensation for the subject matter experts as well as an advisory committee, is generally estimated to be $100,000 per program, although this varies with the length and level of the program. The impact of costs associated with the use of a disciplined process for this purpose represents far more than "savings." A successful program with moderate enrollment of twenty to twenty-five students per year can generate a surplus over direct costs as early as the second year of implementation. However, the ability to avoid launching programs that are not sustainable due to a lack of enrollment, for example, is far more impactful. The "savings" then, relates to preserving the value of a degree to students, the institution's reputation with its public and regulators, and the cost of a "teach out."

Program Evaluation In addition to the ongoing assessment of the process by the New Program Development Committee, each program holds a "postlaunch" analysis at three and six months after the start of a new program to determine whether initial assumptions regarding market potential were correct, whether the curriculum components have been successfully made operational, what early feedback we have from students, and whether the resources needed for successful launch were sufficient and effective. In addition, faculty from each of the institutions also hold an annual assessment of student learning and program effectiveness. New programs are particularly scrutinized for the metrics associated with growth and efficiencies, and recommendations become part of the institution's planning and budgeting cycle for the upcoming year.

All of the institutions affiliated with TCS Education System are currently finalizing their strategic growth plans for the next five years. Crucial information from these plans includes intended new programs for development that are funneled through the new program development process. Institutional consideration of potential programs was supported by extensive market research provided by TCS Education System's Market Research Department and by the "Innovation Acceleration" seminar held earlier in the academic year with all academic leaders within the system to propose, brainstorm, and refine potential program ideas. An additional twenty new programs are anticipated to be in the process within the year.

AN EXPERIMENT IN FOSTERING A CURRICULAR SOCIETY

John Holzhüter

From 2002 to 2007, I was fortunate to lead a remarkable team of teachers, social workers, adult educators, and dedicated volunteers at a large nonprofit (Let's Help, Inc.) in Topeka, Kansas. Our educational programming and services included high school completion, GED, ESL/ELL, and family literacy programming. We also offered employment training and placement services and barrier reduction assistance for students and their parents or guardians. Our lead nonprofit partner (the Winter Center for Restorative Justice) offered additional onsite programming in the areas of restorative mentoring (for students with a juvenile offense record), VoTech projects, work-study initiatives, and a program to help assimilate students who had been in long-term residential foster care. The facilities for the education and lifelong learning department had recently been renovated and included state-of-the-art computer labs and classrooms with ample space and equipment.

The student body was diverse with variable commitment, capabilities, and aspirations. Program participants ranged in age from sixteen to eighty-three and came from a variety of backgrounds. For some, attendance was mandated, either as part of juvenile criminal sentencing or as a requirement to receive state assistance benefits. For others, it was a voluntary return to secondary education ambitions that had been sidelined by unforeseen circumstance. Despite group diversity, the shared sense of a "premature break" in their academic progress forged a strong sense of connection and feelings of shared identity. This common culture of support and engagement, while highly motivational to those endeavoring to complete secondary education (either certificate of general education or diploma), did not extend to or even conceive of participation in higher education. Individual career aspirations had long been replaced by mutual feelings of educational futility.

Dreams of higher education had long since been abandoned as unrealistic. Thinking in terms of J-O-B and a slight increase in wage seemed more prudent and much safer than contemplating long-term career plans. No longer viewed as the first step on the path of higher education, the receipt of a certificate of general education or high school diploma had become the ultimate goal. All drive was set to that calibration, and no measure planned beyond that apex. Once met, the inclination for further study of any kind simply did not occur. What was more, the support systems and social networks of the student-participants shared and reinforced this philosophy. While friends, family members, and coworkers strongly encouraged efforts to complete secondary education, they expressed little faith in the participant's potential success in continuing-education opportunities. The "societal curriculum" ended at precisely the same level that our programming did, right after high school.

Carlos E. Cortés (1979) defines *societal curriculum* as the "massive, ongoing, informal curriculum of family, peer groups, neighborhoods, churches, organizations, occupations, mass media and other socializing forces that 'educate' all of us throughout our lives" (p. 479). We began to realize that a significant shift in the group-thought of societal curriculum was needed. While referrals to tertiary education were available and scholarship or financial aid applications were viable options, these opportunities existed only as a brochure on the wall or a discussion that quickly deteriorated into job placement options and workforce skill development. The tangibility of any type of education outside of the limits of this insular culture seemed impossible to imagine. While student-participants had come to acknowledge the adult education department as a place of educational success, additional educational experiences were linked to other previous external learning opportunities that had led to failure and rejection, either chosen or forced.

In order to change the societal curriculum, the space itself, not just the mindset or the programming, had to become a bridge and a testing ground for postsecondary education. By infusing and extending our programming partnerships, we could begin to prepare students for the transition to college. Such programming and partnership had to encompass some form of higher education coursework that would be offered onsite. Our recent renovations also required that we best utilize the space by providing both day and evening classes and also by extending the course offerings into the community. Opportunities had to be developed, attitudes changed, and behaviors fostered that would drive postsecondary successes and insist that higher learning could be the new goal—without the defined limit of secondary education.

We found a willing partner in Allen County Community College, which describes itself as convenient, affordable, and friendly and prides itself on offering unique and caring learning environments. Allen County and their director of outreach, Dick Allison, were eager to partner and to creatively serve our student-participant population. In the initial stages of our partnership, Allen County began to offer concurrent credit for high school seniors and upper-level GED testing program participants, with these courses offered in our facilities. This familiar environment offered the bridge we sought both in location and in coursework. The program took off, and we expanded by targeting a health emphasis. Allen County offered classes (in our classrooms and later both onsite and on their campus) leading to several certification options: CNA (certified nurse's aide), CMA (certified medical assistance), and HHCA (home health certified aide).

After just the second semester, this programming proved successful as new graduates secured employment in their new fields. We expanded the programming areas to include early childhood education with a focus on paraprofessional training and daycare certification. We allowed building space to be utilized, free of charge, for night classes and other community college, and nonprofit partners offered additional areas of programming. Industry programs became the next natural extension.

InVEST, a school-to-work insurance program that paired GED test preparation student teams with industry professionals and community colleges, provided another avenue for entrance into postsecondary education and also gave the opportunities for job-shadow days, internships, and career experiences. A partnership was developed with the regional FastTrac, an entrepreneurial program, to provide an avenue for postsecondary training to assist potential small business owners in developing organizational and managerial skills and developing thorough and realistic business plans.

Through the cobbling together of these varied postsecondary educational offerings and more specifically by offering the coursework within the established space as well as in offsite campuses, the culture began to shift, and postsecondary education became a feasible and possible goal. The pictures in the brochures and on websites were real; the "college teachers," "college students," "business professionals," and "business owners" were in the building. Successful former GED test students, now in college (Washburn University), began returning to volunteer as tutors and mentors as part of their scholarship requirements (Bonner Scholars, a program of the Corella and Bertram Bonner Foundation). With each success story, higher educational goals became fathomable and even attainable. Students began requesting individual goal-setting plans, which include vocational and entrepreneurial goals. They anticipated that they could do anything as long as they worked hard and had some help. The societal curriculum had evolved to a new status quo. Our building was the place to go if you wanted to learn—anything. We grew more programs and partnerships to ensure that we could offer a little of everything. There were concerns about programming costs, but for the most part, funding kept pace with our rapid expansions.

We financed the programming through a series of grants (primarily the State Adult Basic Education Grant and United Way funding) and "per student" participant subsidies from the State Social Rehabilitation Services. Additional support was garnered through resource and monetary contributions from our educational partners and from encumbered private donations. This generated roughly $600,000 per year and impacted a little over four hundred students. It was a model that worked and worked well. The efforts of partners, teachers, volunteers, and learners had created a space that was viewed as "the place to learn."

It was everything we could have hoped for. I share this because the model is ripe for replication, and it is my ardent hope that it spreads like wildfire to places where past failures create a societal curriculum that squelches student dreams and limits learner's ambitions.

SOCIAL ENTERPRISE PARTNERSHIPS AND INNOVATIVE CTE (CAREER TECHNICAL EDUCATION) PROGRAM DEVELOPMENT

Rosanna Stoll Diaz

Broward College (BC), formerly Broward Community College, serves approximately sixty thousand students at multiple campuses located in southeastern Florida. The college houses the Marine Engineering Management Program that was designed to address a particular community need for a skilled, literate workforce in the tricounty area's (Broward, Miami-Dade, and Palm Beach) significant recreational boating industry. This program illustrates a significant innovation by employing a social enterprise paradigm in the creation of a demand-driven, community-engaged process for development of new CTE programs.

The Marine Engineering Management Program was developed thoughtfully and organically through the diligent and dedicated work of a social enterprise partnership. The partnership that continues to support the Marine Engineering Management Program at BC was the result of the culmination of a series of meetings and conversations conducted over a two-year period. The partnership was led by BC's dean and the Marine Industries Association of South Florida (MIASF), the leading marine industry trade association. Guided by the BC dean and MIASF's executive director and director of membership services, the meetings were attended by BC personnel, MIASF members representing marine businesses and employers, marine industry media, the BC Foundation, and other representatives from interested constituent groups, including Broward County schools and the Broward County Workforce Board.

The program became operational in 2008 and graduated its first class in 2010. About 70 percent of the students who enrolled in the pilot program completed all the technical and academic requirements of the program and graduated with two to three industry certifications. Although the economy in South Florida has experienced the same challenges as many other U.S. markets, program enrollment has grown each year, with a new class of twenty-five students enrolled for fall 2010 with a waiting list for the January 2011 class in place. Funding of major facility expansion remains a challenge. However, due to the success of the program in graduating skilled technicians, the marine business community has committed to underwriting the cost of adding modular classrooms to support expansion of the program's capacity.

The MIASF and BC have worked together in developing and maintaining the program. This collaboration is a continuous process cultivated through monthly advisory board meetings and attendance by advisory board members at marine industry and college-sponsored events. Along with the BC Foundation, MIASF and BC collectively and collaboratively wrote the three-year Community Block Job Training Grant that seeded the program; created the program curriculum; developed the advisory board; identified and hired qualified faculty; promoted the program to the industry and the media; raised private donations of equipment, supplies, and cash; and created additional opportunities through the American Boat and Yacht Council and other concomitant marine organizations.

The program only offers an associate's degree (no certificates) and operates with the assistance of an active program advisory board, which meets regularly. The board contributes to a variety of resources, including technical and fundraising assistance, industry contacts, equipment donations, internship sites, and curriculum development. Each of the primary program partners is represented on the advisory board and actively participates in the program's ongoing development and maintenance.

At the college level, the marine program is housed in the Transportation Department along with associate degree programs from aviation and automotive. All the transportation programs share an administrative assistant and a specialized academic advisor, while the automotive and marine programs are supported by an associate dean along with an advertising and marketing specialist. Finally, the Marine Engineering Management Program employs two full-time instructors, one adjunct instructor and a student lab assistant. Research on the program's genesis and maintenance has been published, and a formal evaluation of the program's performance since its inception is currently being developed. Detailed program information can be found at http://www .broward.edu/marine.

At their core, partnerships are comprised of people, not organizations. The commitment and vision of the people who are involved in the partnership are clearly focused on a common mission-driven goal for all the constituent organizations represented. By focusing on a common program mission that is central to all constituent groups' own organizational missions, all partners have a stake in the successful outcome, and the best interests of the student cohort is served. The program design organically adheres to the social enterprise concepts of innovation, collaboration, sustainability, accountability, and impact in the community that it serves. With institutionally relevant adaptation, this model can be applied to an assortment of CTE programs in a variety of markets. The universal tenets of affordability, open access, and community engagement that are indigenous to the community college mission are decidedly compatible with the social purpose and mission-driven focus of social enterprise and social entrepreneurship concepts.

Social enterprise partnerships provide community colleges an opportunity to increase the reach and intensity of their mission-focused impact on the vast and diverse community of learners whom contemporary community colleges are now engaged in serving. By employing the social enterprise concepts that emerged from the program research, which include sustainability, accountability, and, most importantly, innovation and collaboration, community colleges can develop successful partnerships with local businesses, industry organizations, and other concomitant mission-focused agencies. These partnerships, when developed thoughtfully and organically, can enhance revenue streams, expand reach, and fill a community-based need that is demand driven and socioeconomically relevant to the array of constituent groups in the communities that the colleges serve.

⑫

TECHNOLOGY

Allan M. Hoffman

"To raise new questions, new possibilities, to regard old problems from a new angle, requires creative imagination and marks real advance in science."

—Albert Einstein

THE IMPACT AND PROMISE OF TECHNOLOGY

Technology continues to transform the landscape of tertiary education by reducing accessibility barriers, expanding student services and markets, increasing classroom efficiencies, and informing students' choices as consumers. Not only does it unite people, but it also connects disciplines and institutions and significantly blurs the lines between teacher, student, and entrepreneur. Driven by the educational market and the demands of business, higher education is both a leading inventor and a voracious consumer of cutting-edge technologies. Forced to respond to the frantic pace of globalization, the staggering advancements in communication and information sharing, and the increasingly savvy student-consumers, tertiary institutions must continually ride the technological wave. Teaching and learning processes require constant rethinking to avoid becoming antiquated.

Educational consumers and supporters now demand real-time, cutting-edge instruction with all the gadgets, bells, and whistles. Marketing efforts must merge demands for extensive and transparent institutional reporting with ease and speed of information access. The choice of educational providers is often influenced by available technology and the services offered to maintain and access technology. The availability of student progress data is imperative to ensure the objective benchmarking of learning effectiveness. Students and their advisors look to timely feedback on their academic standing. Administrators are becoming accustomed to real-time results for their assessment of course-level programming and student retention factors. Additionally, the Department of Education mandates that access to a variety of information is afforded to prospective and current students. Schools are required to provide a notice of these student rights under the Family Educational Rights and Privacy Act.

Still, obstacles to technology-based innovations continue to slow the pace of implementation at many institutions of higher learning. A lack of product awareness, technical support, and user training generates faculty reluctance. Students have fears of the security of their personal information and the safety of their personal computers. Tight cash flow and public scrutiny of costs can spook administrators. A consortia-team approach, incorporating multidepartmental members and peers from across institutional jurisdictions, is becoming increasingly more common. Through the utilization of collective experience, best-practice sharing, and the leveraging of combined knowledge, risks are minimized, and costs are shared. Technology is not only serving the learner-consumer but also affording convenience to the instructor and cost benefits and confidence to the intuition as a whole. The following stories highlight success and offer product-based solutions to specific institutional challenges.

NOTEBOOK COMPUTER PROGRAM

William "Bill" Petersen, University of Minnesota, Crookston

William "Bill" Petersen The University of Minnesota, Crookston (UMC), a small campus in the University of Minnesota system with about 1,300 full-time students, offers a variety of applied, career-oriented degree programs. In 1993, UMC became the first four-year institution in the country to provide a notebook computer to every student and faculty member. Computers are obtained on a two-year lease, which ensures that students always have an up-to-date machine not more than two years old. Computers are distributed with a standard load of current software. Loaner machines, onsite warranty service, and complete warranty coverage including accidental damage mean that a student is never without access to a computer. Connectivity is provided everywhere on campus. All classrooms include connectivity and power for everyone along with a projector and a digital imaging camera. In effect, every campus classroom becomes a computer laboratory. Special additional features are included in some classrooms, depending on their design and use. Student technology support is provided through the computer help desk and faculty support through the Center for Teaching, Learning, and Technology. A few major advantages have resulted from this program:

- Equal access to computers is available to all students.
- Identical software makes instruction easier.
- Computers become a primary instructional tool due to constant access. If a student has a computer problem that can't be fixed immediately by the help desk, they are provided a loaner machine.

The primary factors motivating the development of this notebook computer program include the following:

- There was a strong message from employers concerning graduates, that is, wanting good computer skills in their new employees.
- Traditional computer laboratories on campus were all out of date.
- No new funds were available for new computer laboratories.

Although a few colleges at that time had provided computers to select groups of students, UMC was the first college to provide notebook computers to all students and faculty. As a result, UMC had to develop all the associated processes required to implement this program. The total time from the initial concept to the deployment of computers was less than one year, with implementation in fall 1993. The purchase of the initial fleet of computers, renovation of several classrooms, faculty training, development of a new course for student training, and all the associated policies and procedures were developed during that year. The primary costs associated with the project included the cost of the notebook computers, classroom renovations, campus wiring, and the establishment of the computer help desk. The student notebook computer costs were financed through a student technology fee. Other costs were paid through campus budgets.

The primary resistance to implementing the program came in obtaining funding to purchase the initial set of computers. Resistance from faculty was minimal primarily because of the following:

- All faculty members were provided a new notebook computer with current software without any charge to department budgets.
- Students were very excited about the program.
- There was a substantial amount of positive external publicity about the program.

Presently the direct cost of maintaining the notebook computer program, including computer lease costs along with support, is approximately $250 per student per semester. That cost is financed through a $250 per semester student notebook computer fee. There are two important cost savings because of this program:

1. Because everyone has the same model computer with the same load of software, support provided by the UMC computer help desk is far more efficient and requires less staffing than would be required if we did not have the notebook program.
2. Because classrooms are wired or wireless, every classroom becomes a computer laboratory, and there is very minimal need for providing other student computer laboratories.

UMC continually uses a variety of measurements to evaluate student response to the notebook computer program. A few of the results include the following:

- In a survey of new students, the notebook computer program continues as one of the top three reasons students choose to attend UMC.
- In a survey of both UMC and University of Minnesota Twin Cities (UMTC), compared to UMTC students, UMC students had:
  - o fewer technology problems related to hardware and software,
  - o more positive attitudes related to use of educational technology on a variety of questions, and
  - o more positive responses about instructor use of technology.
- EDUCAUSE (a non-profit association whose mission is to advance the effective promotion and use of technology) surveys indicate a more positive response from UMC to questions related to use of educational technology when compared to other campuses of the University of Minnesota, as well as to other institutions.

Additional information about the UMC notebook computer program is available at http://www1.crk.umn.edu/admin/tss/helpdesk/notebooks/index.html.

Although UMC continues to use this program to provide notebook computers to everyone on campus, there have been a number of changes and modifications during the years since the program was implemented. Some of these include the following:

- After the first set, all computers have been leased typically on a two-year lease. Besides ensuring that no computer is more than two years old, this makes it far easier to maintain an up-to-date computer fleet.
- Now all UMC graduates have the option of keeping a notebook computer upon graduation in exchange for a $50 donation to the UMC Alumni Fund.
- A pilot project is underway to investigate the use of convertible tablet computers in place of the traditional notebook computers.
- A new informatics laboratory enriches and opens new horizons for the student notebook educational experience. In the lab, the students are able to use their notebooks to access, retrieve, and analyze data from servers dedicated to Geospatial Information Systems involving applications from a variety of areas. The laboratory

also includes a high-performance, immersive visualization system to which appropriate student-developed notebook programs and applications can be uploaded and used.

IMPROVING STUDENT SUCCESS
THROUGH FREE COMPUTER REPAIR

Michael Bunch

Recent history has shown that computer usage is growing by leaps and bounds in the field of education. Students are now using computers to compose their papers and complete research. Every program at Midstate College is incorporating computer work of one kind or another. Most traditional students get a new computer when they go off to college. At Midstate, we serve the nontraditional student. Many of our students are working adults going back to college to enter a new field. A substantial portion of those students do not have the resources to buy a new computer. They have families to support and rely on federal aid in order to attend school.

In 2002, the Technical Support Department at our college developed a new division, comprised of federal work-study students from the Computer Information Sciences Program. Our federal work-study students gained experience with help desk support and refined their customer service skills. Most of them continued in the support field and obtained new jobs in technical support because of this experience. Our computing services manager oversaw these students as they provided phone support, answered user questions about homework, assisted in virus removal, and performed basic software/hardware troubleshooting.

Prior to the creation of our free computer repair division, many students with serious software and hardware issues were forced to drop classes or even withdraw until they could purchase a new or used computer that was reliable and up to date. Our college serves many students who lack the financial resources to maintain and repair their home computers. Many of our students had computers that were too old to run the latest software and operating systems required for their courses. Many of them have more important things on which to spend money, such as their children and living expenses. We saw a great opportunity to help these students and expand our technicians' experience in customer service, troubleshooting, and computer repair.

Later in 2002, we began allowing eLearning students with major hardware and software issues to bring their computers to campus to see if our support team could help them. We only worked on a few at a time, but we realized quickly that most computers could be fixed in just one day. We realized we were saving each student hundreds of dollars, and this service could really improve retention. We could save good students who really needed help, and after all, we had nothing to lose by trying. We expanded the service to include hardware and software repair for all students, faculty, and staff in 2003.

In the beginning of this program, our technical support staff shared a desk in our library, as we are a small college, and space is always at a premium. There were only a few computers there at any given time, and even though we always had someone on duty in the library, security was a growing issue. When the opportunity became available, we moved the support staff into an office located in the back of the library with lockable storage cabinets to keep laptops secure. Over time, we realized federal work-study students had a high turnover rate, so we decided to add one full-time and one part-time employee to our department. These permanent employees trained the federal work-study students and helped to maintain the knowledge base we were building to track common issues.

The Microsoft campus agreement allows us to upgrade/reinstall operating systems and distribute and install Microsoft Office. We also use a permission request form signed by students to allow us to work on their computers and install software for them. With these processes, we have the ability to reformat the computer and install a new operating system while removing any viruses or spyware on the student's computer. Computers that have a restore partition are reset to the original factory settings unless the system is older and the student requests an upgrade. We always back up the student's personal data before we begin. This process allows them to keep their important files and enables them to start fresh with all the software they need to attend college. Most students only need their documents, pictures, and music backed up and moved onto the new operating system. This process usually requires a copy of the "My Documents" folders and the "Desktop" folder. This process is very simple for saving the data that they need the most.

In 2008, our senior developer created a recordkeeping system to keep track of all incoming support requests. Our current load averages 60 computers every 12 weeks (about 240 computer systems per year). This tracking system allows us to verify a student's schedule, school status, and support history. We are continually building our knowledge base to help the technicians solve issues that we come across frequently. Students are now informed of the free computer repair service during orientation and through the technical support office when requesting support. Students are encouraged to make appointments before bringing in their computers at times when we service a larger number of requests, such as near the beginning of each term. This process allows us to take care of the emergency cases and delay those who just need their systems cleaned up in order to run more efficiently and effectively.

Now in 2010, we have a solid program that has proven invaluable to students, faculty, and staff. This innovative idea, born from one of the basic philosophies and values of Midstate College, "fostering student success," continues to grow. It offers services for users that directly and indirectly impact their current and future success. Our lessons in adapting technical support have turned into a win/win situation for all.

TRANSPARENCY BY DESIGN: SPEARHEADING CONSUMER INFORMATION FOR ADULTS

Michael J. Offerman

Transparency by Design is the first and only national consumer-information and accountability initiative exclusively focused on adults who are prospective students of higher education. The most important aspect of Transparency by Design—and the major difference from other voluntary consumer-information and accountability efforts—is our reporting of program-learning outcomes. Adults want to know what a program can do for them in real and immediate terms. Today Transparency by Design is a diverse mix of regionally accredited, adult-serving programs or institutions delivering higher education at a distance.

The institutions and programs participating in Transparency by Design are often unfamiliar to the prospective adult student. They most often don't have sports teams to capture headlines. Some don't have physical campuses. As such, it's especially important to these programs and institutions to spearhead consumer education and accountability for proving and reporting on the effectiveness of their programs in ways that go beyond what has been higher education's tradition. We have focused on clearly articulating the intended learning outcomes for each program, how we assess whether the outcomes have been achieved, and the results of our assessments. The initiative publishes program-level learning outcomes and how well graduates demonstrate achievement of those outcomes at Transparency by Design's consumer-information site, www.CollegeChoicesForAdults.org.

Adult consumers want information. We live in an era of rapidly expanding educational options, often provided by new or relatively unknown institutions. While the marketing of these options proliferates, they lack relevant, comparative consumer information. Anyone today can go online to research and compare products and services, prices and warranties, and customer ratings. Why should higher education be any different? It often has been! Adults seeking a college program are bombarded with promotional messages from colleges and universities. They may find themselves buried in too many choices to analyze individually. It may seem daunting to sift through the marketing messages to find information essential to making an informed decision. Adults who are considering higher education want to know whether their investment in education will pay off in terms of career goals and promotions. Will they fit in? Can they succeed? What will this program enable them to know and do? What have other students who have completed this program experienced?

Transparency by Design, with its College Choices for Adults website, is about providing adults with verifiable, objective, comparative information they can use in their decision making. Providing meaningful consumer information for adults requires transparency and the disclosure of information at unprecedented levels that together constitute a new level of accountability. Those of us on the frontlines have come to appreciate firsthand how difficult it is to achieve accountability and transparency in higher education. Fear can set in as the old paradigms fall aside. The very idea of capturing and publishing actual learning outcomes raises the ire of some and creates a sense of dread for others. For the former, this is a philosophical difference. For the latter, the fear is about publishing learning outcomes that are less than impressive or, worse still, less than satisfactory.

Transparency by Design institutions and programs have discovered that our work to identify the best metrics for informing consumers also drives internal improvement. Putting data out for the public is a scary proposition and not one that we take lightly. It takes courage—and all of us in Transparency by Design have been asked if we are crazy to publish such detailed results. It's true that presenting this data carries risk. But it also holds the potential for power: Sharing information for the use of the consumer results in public transparency about the bad as well as the good and results in efforts to become better. We're trying to look at assessment of learning because that allows each of us to improve and be accountable. All of us attest that we have made improvements to our programs and institutions after publishing our results at the College Choices for Adults website.

Transparency by Design chose WCET (Western Cooperative for Educational Telecommunications), a division of the Western Interstate Commission for Higher Education, to provide quality assurance on the data reported by the member institutions and to publish the consumer information website. Transparency by Design is funded by a grant to WCET from Lumina Foundation for Education and annual dues from member institutions. Annual dues for July 2010 through June 2011 range from $1,250 to $5,500 based on the institution's student enrollment, type of membership, and whether the membership is new or a renewal.

Participation in Transparency by Design helps member institutions by building credibility through transparent consumer information. Information on the Transparency by Design initiative, including principles of good practice, a list of participating institutions, and membership information, is online at www.TransparencyByDesign.org.

We're proud to say that we are taking transparency to new levels. Transparency by Design gives its members the opportunity to reach adult prospective students with important consumer information through an independent venue that provides quality assurance. Transparency by Design institutions are asking common questions of their alumni. For what is believed to be the first time in higher education, we are presenting comparisons of alumni feedback across institutions and programs. All are sharing information about student engagement, core learning outcomes, program expectations, and results.

Openly sharing evidence of effectiveness gives adult consumers valuable information to help them weigh the merits of a program or institution. It is worth noting that Transparency by Design does not collect leads for its member institutions or serve as a marketing outlet for them. College Choices for Adults is strictly an information-only site.

13

FACILITIES

"The essential part of creativity is not being afraid to fail."

—Edwin H. Land

ENVIRONMENT MATTERS!

Studies continue to validate that the conditions of the learning environment greatly impact the success of the learning. Student retention surveys have shown that uncomfortable classrooms and drafty dorm rooms tend to do more than just distract. They are listed as the primary reasons some students decide to drop out, especially among low-income students. While insect infestations, poor lighting, and accessibility challenges are now uncommon in public places, they remain a sad reality at many of our nation's tertiary institutions. Often storage space is a commodity and once-usable teaching space is now home to unused equipment. Aging buildings are overdue for retrofit or rebuilding. Outdated furnace and air conditioning units consume massive amounts of energy and struggle to perform as required.

But there is hope. Facilities, historically overlooked and underfunded, are finally getting much-needed attention. The emphasis on "going green," increasing enrollment numbers, and raising student expectations on personal space and the environment in general are drawing innovation to facility conditions previously overlooked or merely taken for granted. The terms *energy conservation, emissions,* and *renewable energy* absent from facility improvement proposals since the late 1970s are again in common use. Private colleges are finding that students are no longer satisfied with hand-me-downs or government surplus. Public institutions are facing more scrutiny for cost efficiencies from state and federal funders. For-profit schools are looking at how facilities impact return on investment.

Facility managers are getting permission to rethink and reevaluate the band-aid approaches to maintenance funded from the annual operations budget. Institution administrators are exploring the costs and social benefits of new technologies and contemplating capital campaigns and incentive funding. Progressive institutions are looking for ways to manage space, plant, and equipment to provide sustainable amenities in resourceful ways. The following success stories prove that creativity, effort, and emphasis spent on facility improvements can afford exponential benefits to all institutional stakeholders.

CREATING CLASSROOMS WE'RE PROUD OF

Barbara A. Farley

After years of deferred maintenance and lack of accountable management, classroom facilities at Augsburg College had reached a new low in 2006. Sporadic investments in classroom technology had only made the contrasts starker: Spaces with advanced presentation technology might lack a functioning clock or have unworkable lighting. Many classrooms had mismatched chairs or had become dumping grounds for unwanted items from nearby offices—a stray file cabinet or a broken coffeemaker. Much of the furniture, like tablet-arm chairs, looked to be from a high school and not suited for the adult learner population that now comprised nearly half of the student body. Even the new technology setups varied so widely that faculty had to learn systems room by room. As Augsburg faculty gave deep consideration to learning styles or new developments in pedagogy, there was no sign of such progress in the experience of Augsburg classrooms.

In spring 2006, the dean of the college gathered a working group of key stakeholders from across campus—advising, facilities, registrar, information technology, library, center for teaching and learning, student affairs, and academic affairs. With two building projects looming, this committed group of professionals saw a key opportunity to do things differently. New literature on the importance of learning spaces had emerged to inform the design of great new classrooms. The literature also gave importance to informal learning spaces—the important spaces outside of the classroom had so often been an afterthought.

Meeting over four months, the group created design standards drawn not only from the new literature on learning space design but also based on Chickering and Gamson's *Seven Principles of Good Practice in Undergraduate Education.* The principles stated that Augsburg's campus spaces should encourage contact between students and faculty, encourage reciprocity and cooperation among students, encourage active learning, and respect diverse talents and ways of learning. The principles informed decisions for new building projects and guided a new institutional investment in classroom spaces. Standards were created to address classroom presentation technology, mobile furniture, lighting, and quality aesthetics.

Augsburg's existing classroom spaces were assessed against a rating system based on the principles, and the project became the 16 Classrooms Project, referring to the investment needed to move our classrooms portfolio into an acceptable midpoint of the rating system. The group also recommended a new structure for the ongoing management and support of classrooms to include a new budget built on a replacement-cycle funding model. A new position was created—the teaching and learning spaces liaison— a "classroom champion" responsible for the classroom budget, a small student staff, the support and maintenance of the spaces, and the strategic scheduling of the spaces.

Even in its first-phase launch, the 16 Classrooms Project became one of the most well-received investments by students and faculty: All new and renovated classrooms received a ceiling-mounted data projector, in-ceiling speakers, DVD/VCR unit, PC desktop, and a laptop connection all controlled by a standard simple push-button control panel. All furniture has wheels, and one table is wheelchair accessible. All rooms have several wall-mounted whiteboards on the front and side walls as well as mobile whiteboards in some rooms. Carpet, paint, and lighting are also evaluated and replaced if needed.

Not only did Augsburg's facilities for teaching and learning see a sudden, dramatic improvement, but also Augsburg's new management of classrooms drives continuous improvement and ongoing deliberation with faculty and students. With a dedicated budget for classroom maintenance and improvement, more rooms each year have been outfitted with the technology, furniture, and design aesthetics laid out in the design principles. Feedback is gathered annually through a campus survey to assess how the teaching and learning spaces perform as well as how the support for those spaces performs when measured against the design principles. The rating system developed for the 16 Classrooms Project is revisited annually to determine progress in moving all campus classrooms to the highest level of quality. The faculty have broadly embraced the changes to the classrooms across campus and strongly desire teaching in rooms that meet the design principles. In particular, mobile furniture allows them to adapt the room to their teaching style on a given day. It is not uncommon to see a room in several configurations over the course of a day.

ASPIRE: MAINTAINING ACCURATE SPACE DATA TO ACHIEVE AN OPTIMAL ASSIGNMENT OF SPACE

Donna Michalek

Accounting for Space, People, Indexes, Research, and Equipment (ASPIRE) maintains the accurate data on space and facilities that is required for public safety, classroom scheduling, facilities and maintenance, energy conservation, computer networking and telephony, and various other applications. It also satisfies regulatory requirements as an integral part of the process of assigning institutional space into Office of Management and Budget (OMB; a cabinet-level office and the largest office within the executive office of the president of the United States) Circular A-21 functional categories based on space use. ASPIRE was developed because crucial space data were in a state of disarray. Prior to the development and implementation of ASPIRE, twelve major space databases or data repositories existed on campus. The data were not consistent from database to database or in some instances with physical reality. A clear authoritative database did not exist, which could mean that if one database was updated, others were not. The databases were not user friendly, which contributed to the inaccuracy of the data because data entry was difficult. Finally, engineering drawings were not always updated as buildings were modified.

The project took eighteen months from the time of problem definition through implementation of the Web tool. This included in-house development of the "space software tool." Rollout of the tool to the campus community took place after this time period. Training and continued improvement based on user feedback is continuous, as is updating the database. The cost of implementing ASPIRE was that of personnel time only, including but not limited to the meeting time for the Academic Quality Improvement Program (AQIP) action project team, development of the software, creating a space coordinator in facilities management by reassignment of duties, and development of training materials.

No resistance was faced during the development phase of ASPIRE, as all involved clearly understood the benefits of the new tool. During the implementation phase, some resistance was encountered from the wider campus community, who were concerned about the time required by each unit to update their space data. Each unit was requested to appoint a space coordinator who would be responsible for checking and updating the data on a regular basis. This was an additional task that had to be performed by an individual who may already be fully utilized, as many units operate with a lean staff. This resistance was reduced by making the task of checking and updating the database as user friendly and easy as possible. Seeking continual feedback from users and implementing their suggestions on an ongoing basis has also reduced this resistance.

The cost and savings are entirely in personnel time and have not been calculated. The motivation for implementing ASPIRE was not to save money but to provide accurate data on space, and therefore cost savings have not been determined.

The two major means of checking the performance of ASPIRE are by feedback from the users and from the tool itself. The software tool is designed to issue exception reports if a data discrepancy is detected. This is an indication that the tool is not working as intended.

The ASPIRE website is located at www.admin.mtu.edu/space. Any print documents can be found at this website location. The University Space Committee uses ASPIRE to maximize space utilization in providing quality service to our students, faculty, and staff. As previously mentioned, it is also an integral part of the process of assigning institutional space into functional categories based on use as is required to be in compliance with OMB Circular A-21. Other uses are unit specific but include interrogating the system concerning space utilization (room occupants, efforts of occupants, research sponsors, and expenditures of room occupants) and equipment locations, running error reports to discover inconsistencies and exceptions in space data, and auditing and executive management for planning purposes.

CARBON-NEUTRAL AQIP (EXCERPTED FROM FINAL REPORT, DECEMBER 2008)

Margaret "Peg" Gale

The Carbon Neutral AQIP project was developed to better integrate Michigan Tech's goals of sustainability with our education and research efforts now and into the future. Margaret R. (Peg) Gale, dean of the School of Forest Resources and Environmental Science, and John W. Sutherland, director of the Sustainable Futures Institute, co-chaired this project. The goal of this project was to develop a process using carbon as the metric to improve Michigan Tech's use of energy and materials and enhance our educational and research programs. We focused on infrastructure plans to reduce carbon emissions toward neutrality and developed a model to estimate our carbon emissions and offsets and the detailed process by which we can begin to integrate Tech's goal of carbon neutrality into our educational programs. We also suggested certain actions to help us achieve the final goals of carbon neutrality and the integration of these concepts into all we do at Michigan Tech.

As a higher education institution, we recognize that it is our responsibility to lead by example and to initiate changes in human behavior through our educational and research programs with the aim of creating a more sustainable society for future generations. The formation of the Presidential Committee on Environmental Sustainability in 2001 produced a comprehensive document, *Greenprint for Environmental Sustainability in Campus Operations and Activities*, which recommended actions the university could take to reduce our energy use. In 2003, the Sustainable Futures Institute was formed, whose mission is centered around research and graduate education on sustainability. Many of our educational programs concentrate their instructional efforts on sustainability with emphases on carbon cycles (see www.mtu.edu/sfhi/educational). Moreover, several research centers at Michigan Tech promote sustainability education, research in carbon cycles, and the effect of society on this cycle, addressing the policy, engineering, ecological, economic, business, cultural, and sustainable community dimensions of four thematic areas—air, water, energy, and materials. Our Environmental Sustainability Committee (ESC) also coordinates community outreach and educational programs and has led several campus initiatives seeking to improve Tech's collective ecological footprint.

While most universities have taken the approach of reducing their emissions by reducing specific high-emitting components, such as purchased electricity, they are not taking a holistic approach to the linking of individual decisions with the goal of reducing the university's emissions and making the campus a sustainable community. Therefore, we embarked on a project to estimate Michigan Tech's carbon emissions and sequestration potential for various components and to subsequently develop a coordinated process to reduce our total emissions now and in the future. This project not only aimed at reducing the university's carbon emissions through a coordinated framework but was also directed at communicating our progress and accomplishments as they occur. We believe a coordinated process for reducing carbon emissions should be embedded in all our scholarly and operational efforts. We therefore used the AQIP to structure a more data-based and action-directed program for improvement to help us to focus on the areas where we can make the biggest strides in accomplishing our general goal of "carbon neutrality."

Being carbon neutral refers to neutral (zero) net-carbon release or zero net-carbon emissions brought about by balancing the amount of carbon released into the atmosphere with the amount sequestered.

Many universities and communities are starting to evaluate carbon neutrality through the use of carbon-accounting models. One such model is the Clean Air–Cool Planet (CA–CP) Campus Carbon Calculator (www .cleanair-coolplanet.org). Often universities use certain building-design standards that hope to reduce emissions.

We chose the CA–CP Campus Carbon Calculator to account for our carbon emissions and help us in the future to determine if we are approaching carbon neutrality by the choices we make. We are using this model largely to establish a baseline for present carbon emissions. The CA–CP Excel spreadsheet fundamentally provides a framework for summarizing, reporting, and reconciling all of the scope areas and thus is an accounting system. We evaluated Michigan Tech's carbon footprint at two levels or scopes. Initial estimates of Tech's CO_2 emissions for the 2008 fiscal year were estimated to be 76,904 metric tons of eCO_2 with 6,892 metric tons of eCO_2 sequestered. Our net CO_2 emissions for the 2008 fiscal year were estimated to be 70,012 metric tons of eCO_2. The largest contribution to our total carbon emissions is from purchased electricity—close to half of our emissions.

The project proposed a process for incorporating campus carbon footprint reduction into our educational and research efforts. It begins with a general overview of the process, then provides a more-detailed explanation of each of the tasks that collectively define the continuous improvement process to be implemented annually to identify, plan, and then pursue carbon footprint reduction project activities. It also describes how students and the campus as a whole are to be involved.

After establishing a university environmental policy, the executive team would update the policy and aspects or performance measures as the first step in an annual continuous improvement process. In addition to revisiting the policy and aspects every year, the executive team annually must define the improvement targets (e.g., 5 percent reduction in carbon footprint) and objectives (e.g., reduce the energy losses in university housing). The next step is planning improvement projects, such as a Green Campus Enterprise, and defining targets and project goals for academic and nonacademic units, followed by selection of projects to implement. A sustainability coordinator would be named to oversee the carbon reduction process. The challenges we face in the near and far future are: (1) establishing the significant annual event to generate interest in the project, (2) maintaining the continuous process of communication, and (3) effectively changing our culture to reduce Michigan Tech's energy use. The complete report is available at www.admin.mtu.edu/admin/prov/aqip/AQIP%20 Carbon_Neutral%20Final%20Report.pdf.

III

PUTTING IT ALL TOGETHER

Allan M. Hoffman

Individuals and organizations tend to seek innovative approaches that fall within their value systems and correspond to their understanding of current problems or needs. Uncomfortably, this often involves the rejection of popular alternatives as inefficient, ineffective, or impractical and approaching problem solving in a nonlinear way. These concepts of exploration, which professors work to instill in their students, must be demonstrated and nurtured by administrators in their interactions with the educators and staff they lead. New and novel approaches, no matter how potentially promising, are commonly haunted by the specters of uncertain outcomes and fears of negative perception. By developing a culture that allows for risk taking and creating a climate that fosters multidisciplinary discussion and transdisciplinary collaboration, leaders can minimize the perceived threat of "risk." Not only has this philosophy been demonstrated to increase feelings of job satisfaction and reduce turnover, it has the additional benefits of modeling the harmonizing of personal characteristics and of illustrating a balance between authoritative and collective power concepts.

Henry Armand Giroux describes an educational philosophy as "critical pedagogy." According to Giroux, this philosophy "signals how questions of audience, voice, power, and evaluation actively work to construct particular relations between teachers and students, institutions and society, and classrooms and communities. . . . Pedagogy in the critical sense illuminates the relationship among knowledge, authority, and power" (Giroux, 1991, p. 30). The incorporation of this concept, with rampant staff and leadership innovation, affords a progressive environment that ensures even large and established institutions can nimbly and successfully embrace change. It also helps combat the fatigue sometimes brought on by the tenure system through an invigorated connection between staff involvement and participation in a living and topical institutional mission.

Commitment to a culture of continual improvement can offer motivation to long-time employees and mentorship to newcomers. It remains, however, the responsibility of institutional leaders to find new ways to nurture the asset of staff in ways that mirror or exceed practices now common in the business sector. This provides proof that all organizational levels are committed to process improvement and that people are of equal value as process. Opportunities targeted may be improving or eliminating systems considered cumbersome or bothersome, proposing less-intensive and more-user-friendly ways of documentation, or the incorporation of technology. The time spent by leaders in the design of systems that reinforce the value of the individual and worth of the team buttress top-down commitment to efficient critical pedagogy and emphasize the tangible value of systemwide innovation. In the following chapters, we look at innovative aspects and approaches that target the broader issues of staff efficacy, motivation, and locus of control.

14

MOTIVATING SUCCESS

"Discovery consists of seeing what everybody has seen and thinking what nobody has thought."

—Albert von Szent-Gyorgy

WHAT MOTIVATES THE HIGHER ED PROFESSIONAL? IT'S *MORE* THAN MONEY—IT *HAS* TO BE! WHAT MOTIVATES THE STUDENT? IT'S *MORE* THAN THE CLASS CREDIT—IT *SHOULD* BE!

Russell J. Watson

As a higher education professional, have you ever attended a series of meetings for a committee and looked back over the series and asked, "Have we accomplished anything over these past months?" I've thought that more times than once, many more times. As an instructor in a general education course, have you ever wondered why some students are eagerly motivated and others show up only in body but not mind? With a degree in psychology, I can explain a small part of this through motivation, drive, passion, and a few related constructs. What remains are still tens of person-hours spent in mechanical meetings and the occasional appearance of some mechanical students in classes. Is there an academic defibrillator to spark a breath of life into the gray field of meetings and that can do the same to some lifeless faces of students? I think I've found one.

What I observed in a variety of meetings is that professionals of similar behavioral styles (defined as DISC or MBTI terms) either worked effectively together or not, and those of very different styles either got along or not. The bottom line: Behavioral style didn't seem to be the major predictor of success in working teams. Some other dynamic was at work here. The operative dynamic that clearly emerged as crucial to a team's success was the dynamic of *values*. Behavioral style describes *how* one does their job. Terms used to describe *behavioral style* include *type*, *preferences*, *traits*, and *temperament*, among others. All of these terms more closely describe work behaviors and attempt to illuminate *how* one does his or her job or goes about day-to-day activities.

Values illuminate *why* one does his or her job; it is the wins, drives, and rushes as he or she performs duties. When *values* are understood, appreciated, and respected, we find a substantial reduction in on-the-job conflicts between people and teams. We also find substantially increased levels of motivation, especially when participants are offered tasks that amplify specific values drives, that is, when the task offered is in line with one's intrinsic motivation. Interestingly, this process doesn't involve any member of the team necessarily changing what he or she does, nor does it involve any team changing its methods or direction. This remarkable reduction in perceived conflict and increase in level of activity and interest is achieved through an awareness of what drives one's behavior. Those behavioral drive factors are one's *values*, and six or seven values clearly emerge as common across a variety of workplace dimensions (see table 14.1). There are no "right" or "wrong" values positions in the seven listed in table 14.1; there are simply *different* positions.

Values-Driven Students   I'd like to tell you a story about a student named Mark. Some years ago he was in my psychology class, doing fine academically but questioning his future job role. He was an accounting major, and he didn't want to work for a "big eight" firm. (It might be "big five" now or, at the printing of this book, "big three.") I started asking him questions about his values, or drives or motivators, in a side-

14.1. Behavioral Drive Factors

Value/Motivator	Drive for
Theoretical	Knowledge
Economic	Money and resources
Individualistic	Uniqueness
Altruistic	Helping others
Political	Power and independence
Regulatory	Structure and order
Aesthetic	Form, harmony, and balance

door manner. I asked him what magazines he read on a regular basis. He quickly answered *Sports Illustrated*; he specifically added not just the January swimsuit edition. He began a litany of his favorite teams, some of which I'd not heard of before. I asked him to realize that every major sports team doesn't have an accountant; they have a complete accounting department. I suggested that he work with the co-op office at the college to see if he could arrange an internship with one of the teams.

He sent seven letters to his favorite teams. He received three responses. Two teams said, "No, thanks." One team said that they didn't have an internship program, but that was only because no one had ever asked about one. They suggested that he write them a proposal. He did. Mark was accepted as the first accounting department summer intern with a major professional sports team. Within a few short questions, Mark was able to merge his academic major with his values and passions and obtain on-the-job experience in the field. When students are able to make a values or motivation connection between their academic field and their intrinsic motivation, magical things happen.

Values-Driven Colleges   In any college or university, successful teams contain a variety of behavioral styles and values drives. However, winning teams demonstrate at least two (and sometimes three) values drives in common between their members. What this says is that members of winning teams have certain values on which they can at least *in part* agree. Those areas where values differ are usually neutralized upon the identification or understanding of the values position in a climate of mutual respect. I've observed (and led) some amazing values-driven teams and committees. If it's a student outcomes assessment committee and there's research to be done, those with the higher "theoretical" scores willingly jump into the project. If there's a budget snag, those with the higher "economic" scores dive in to find a solution. If we're hosting a conference, those with the higher "altruistic" scores volunteer to make the experience user friendly for everyone.

Activity on values clearly demonstrates that when understanding the values drives and strengths offered by each member of the team, co-operation increases, and so does "discretionary effort." In addition, we can obtain enormous insight with a college by exploring the collective values of specific teams and then further expand this insight by rolling upward and enlightening college norms by aggregating team data. This information is of crucial importance and insight when colleges examine their mission, vision, and goal statements in light of their collective values. No one is asked to change their behavioral style or their values, but they are asked to at least in part agree on certain values and accept that other values positions may differ. The result is a college propelled by intrinsically motivated teams ready to proactively meet the future as it arrives rather than watch the future pass by.

There are a variety of solid tools in the marketplace, and many of them offer academic discounts for colleges and student organizations. As many of these tools are changing and improving, by press time there may be updated resources. If the information herein strikes a chord or interest, please feel free to contact me at tarconinc@aol.com or (630) 554-1200, and I'll provide you with a list of resources.

THE SUPERIOR EDGE—HELPING STUDENTS— AND HELPING OUR COMMUNITY

Rachel Harris and David Bonsall

The Superior Edge encompasses a wide range of in- and out-of-class-room experiences that provide Northern Michigan University (NMU) students with a distinct advantage by better preparing them for careers, graduate school, and life as engaged citizens. The Superior Edge provides students with experiences that complement and personalize the learning taking place in the classroom. The program has four goals that relate to four "edges." The first edge is the citizenship edge, and the goal is that students become engaged, involved citizens. The leadership edge is the second edge, and it is anticipated that students grow as competent, ethical, and effective leaders. The diversity edge's goal is that students develop a world view and better understand and appreciate diversity. The real-world edge permits students to develop the ability to relate theory to practice.

The requirements for each of the edges is that students complete one hundred hours of approved activities and submit a two- to three-page reflection paper that demonstrates how the students met the outcomes for each edge. Students completing all four edges and writing a reflection paper that synthesizes all of their activities are acknowledged as achieving the Superior Edge. Students who participate receive a Superior Edge transcript from the registrar's office documenting their participation in the program. These transcripts are sent whenever a student requests an academic transcript.

There were two primary motivating factors for developing the Superior Edge. The first was to help fulfill NMU's mission that NMU *challenges its students, faculty, staff and alumni to strive for excellence, both inside and outside the classroom, and to become outstanding citizens and leaders.* The second motivating factor was to provide a mechanism for students to document and be recognized for value-added activities that contributed to their professional and personal growth. It took approximately one year to develop the program and begin the pilot phase of implementation. A Value-Added Activities Task Force consisting of faculty, staff, and students began meeting in November 2004 with the following charges: recommending types of experiences and activities that should be included, naming the initiative, developing a record-keeping system, developing a means of assessing quality, determining appropriate promotional and marketing activities, and identifying the required level of support. These tasks were completed during the 2004–2005 academic year. In fall 2005, appropriate staff and administration members were identified, and the pilot program was developed for implementation in the winter 2006 semester.

The purpose of the pilot program was to test the electronic portfolio that was used to record hours and types of activities, determine the clarity of the program's expectations, determine if the developed expectation of one hundred hours for each edge was realistic and reasonable, and develop additional promotional materials. The Superior Edge was piloted in the winter 2006 semester with one hundred volunteer

students. The implementation of the pilot program was guided by the
Superior Edge Task Force, which consisted of faculty, staff, administrators, and students. Following the pilot program, the Superior Edge Task
Force was retired, and the Superior Edge Advisory Committee was
formed. The advisory committee, consisting of faculty, staff, administrators, and students, monitors the program to determine if it meets the
program's goals and outcomes.

The goal for the 2006–2007 academic year was to enroll five hundred students. By November 2006, 645 students had enrolled in the
program. By the end of April 2007, 959 students (approximately 10
percent of the student body) were participating in the program. These
students have logged more than 75,600 hours, while 19 students have
successfully completed the Superior Edge (all four edges), and a total
of 127 individual edges have been completed. The chairperson of the
task force received released time for two semesters ($6,000). The Web
design time was cost neutral, as it was completed by a student volunteer. Pilot program expenses from January through June 2006 totaled
approximately $50,000; these expenses included student labor, office
supplies, room rentals, equipment, office furniture, postage, telephone,
advertising, and promotional pieces.

Some of our major stakeholders had reservations about this program
when it was first introduced. It was difficult to convince some members
of our faculty to promote this program to their students; students, they
said, were already too busy with other activities. Administrators were
initially reluctant to provide adequate funding for this as-yet-untested
program. Students did not initially sign up for the program because it
was not sufficiently advertised to them. Finally, some faculty expressed
reservations about integrating the Superior Edge into the curriculum.

To overcome these points of resistance, the "champions" of the
program described the Superior Edge in multiple forums that were
open to the entire campus community. Their experiences began to
convince others of the program's value. Industry and community leaders also commented in public presentations on how much they valued
our students volunteering in the myriad of community venues in which
our students participated. One industry leader noted that his review
of resumes from college students all had good GPAs. The Superior
Edge, alternatively, provided our students with a means of distinguish-

ing themselves on their resumes. Our administration noted that the program provided recognition for student activities in which many of them were already engaging. They listened to the community leaders who said that our students had an advantage upon graduation in obtaining meaningful employment. They also noted that the program seemed to enhance recruitment and retention. Our extensive marketing of the program at freshmen orientation, on our website, and by word of mouth resulted in many more students taking part in the program than we initially anticipated. Finally, our faculty senate and the university registrar collaborated to designate certain courses in the curriculum as fulfilling an "academic service learning" mission, which became a part of official NMU transcripts.

The annual cost to run Superior Edge is approximately $200,000. The staffing includes one director, one clerical worker, one graduate assistant, and three student employees. Other expenses include promotional expenses, events and activities, office supplies, telephones and computers, recognition, and travel dollars for conference presentations.

We have heard from several high school students that the Superior Edge attracted them to NMU. We believe that the Superior Edge Program has helped recruit students, and we are in the process of trying to determine hard data regarding number of students recruited to NMU because of this program. We are also exploring the program's effect on retention. Qualitative feedback suggests that the Superior Edge gets students involved and connected on campus and in the community, enhancing retention.

Four components have been measured to determine the effectiveness of the program: the student's reflection papers, student enrollment in the program, edge completion, and community impact.

1. Comments from the students' reflection papers: Each of the edges has a list of outcomes that are addressed in the reflection papers. Students must demonstrate in their papers that they have met the objectives of the edge. These are evaluated by the staff in the Superior Edge office to determine if the outcomes have been met.
2. Student enrollment in the program: Our database reports the numbers of students enrolled in each edge, and it is being refined to identify who participates in the program. Factors that will be

evaluated include the student's class standing, major, and demographic characteristics to determine the type of student most likely to participate. This information will be utilized to identify factors that will be successful in targeting students who choose not to participate.

3. Edge completion: Currently the only data collected are the numbers of students who have completed one or more edges. The program's mission is to *provide NMU students with a distinct advantage for preparing them for careers, graduate school and life as engaged citizens*. It is important to determine if this mission is being met and if the evaluation is being targeted to students who participated in the program and have or are graduating. Students who completed "edges" have provided qualitative feedback that the program has assisted in their development and with their job searches and/or graduate school admission. The effect of the Superior Edge transcript on job searches and/or graduate school admission is also being evaluated.

4. Community impact: We have data indicating the impact of volunteer hours in the community. As stated previously, in just one academic year, more than 75,600 hours of activities have been documented. Currently, data from community agencies are being collected. Areas being evaluated include the strengths and weaknesses of the program, the ways the program could be improved, and strategies to enhance community involvement.

The Superior Edge Program is described on the Web at www.nmu.edu/superioredge. Additionally, students who are admitted to NMU are sent an invitation to participate in the Superior Edge Program. The letter explains the program and provides the website for students to review and sign up for the program. There is also a bookmark that is distributed to students during campus visits and college fairs that contains information about the program and the website. During orientation, students receive a presentation on the program and are given the dates of the Superior Edge orientation sessions that are scheduled throughout the semester at different times and places. The Superior Edge Program is extensively advertised to incoming and current students. In practice, students participate in the various edges and record their time per edge.

The program has enhanced town/gown relationships for the university, as our students are volunteering in many local agencies. Student participation becomes a part of an official NMU transcript, providing our students with an advantage upon graduation. Finally, quantitative data from student testimonials suggest that our students gain immense personal satisfaction from program participation.

15

BUILDING THE CAPACITY FOR CHANGE THROUGH INNOVATION

Minnesota State Colleges and Universities
Linda L. Baer and James H. McCormick

"The innovation point is the pivotal moment when talented and motivated people seek the opportunity to act on their ideas and dreams."

—W. Arthur Porter

"Innovate to meet current and future educational needs."

—*Designing the Future*

The Minnesota State Colleges and Universities System provides an environment that is based on innovative approaches to higher education. Innovation in higher education includes the development or adoption of new or existing ideas for the purpose of improving policies, programs, practices, or personnel. Fifteen years ago, the Minnesota State Colleges and Universities emerged from three distinctive systems: the Technical College System, the Community College System, and the State University System. The state legislature mandated this merger with the intention that through this new structure of governance, students, communities, and the state would be better served. The merger included expectations of increased efficiency and effectiveness among and between campuses due to the coordinating approach of a single governing board, a unified strategic and capital plan, and improved credit transfer.

This structure provided the foundation for moving the higher education institutions toward working together in ways they previously had not to improve student access, opportunity, and success.

INNOVATION: STRATEGIC VISIONING AND PLANNING

In 2002, a Citizens Advisory Commission named by the board of trustees issued a report titled *Access to Success*, which made recommendations to focus on access, workforce and economic development, information technology, metropolitan area planning, and accountability. Following that report, the board approved a system strategic plan, *Designing the Future*, which was based on the Citizens Advisory Commission and extensive visits across the state. The board of trustees developed a strategic plan in 2002, which focused on four key strategic directions: access and opportunity, high-quality programs and services, regional and community development, and integrating the system. The plan was developed using input from listening sessions across the state held at each of the thirty-two campuses. A planning task force was developed and included trustees, presidents, and vice chancellors to compile and develop the plan.

The system mission and vision provided the foundation for maximizing the public investment in higher education. The mission states that the *Minnesota State Colleges and Universities system of distinct and collaborative institutions offers higher education that meets the personal and career goals of a wide range of individual learners, enhances the quality of life for all Minnesotans, and sustains vibrant economies throughout the state.* The supporting vision statement supports the long-range view by stating that the Minnesota State Colleges and Universities system will enable the people of Minnesota to succeed by providing the most accessible, highest value education in the nation."

In 2006, the plan was revisited with the major addition of a strategic goal that supported innovation for current and future educational needs. The board believed that a culture of innovation could strengthen the ability of our colleges and universities to work together and meet the expectations of students. Innovation would be crucial to identify efficient ways to enable all Minnesotans to complete some form of higher education. The governing board designated innovation goals that included building organizational capacity for change to meet future challenges and removing barriers to innovation and responsiveness; rewarding and supporting institutions, administrators, faculty, and staff for innovations that advance excellence and efficiency; and hiring and developing leaders who would initiate and support innovation throughout the system.

The strategic planning process recently was updated by the board of trustees. A fifth strategic direction was added addressing the need to find sustainable models for the future. The underlying goals related to financial viability, and the addition of other goals related to student transfer and success; faculty, staff, and student engagement; global workforce issues; and structures and technologies to support transformative innovation. Worthy of note, too, the system office of academic and student affairs division designated a unit for academic innovation, which provided outstanding support to the exploration, launching, and sustaining of new ideas. The exhibit (see figure 15.1) was developed by the division. It identifies the foundation, pillars, and building blocks to innovation from a system to campus perspective, beginning with the understanding that change requires a coordinated approach among programs, services, policies, and tools.

INNOVATION: INVESTING IN UNDERREPRESENTED STUDENTS

A key action that supports innovation is the focus on access, opportunity, and success. A Chancellor's Initiative Program supported the piloting of incentive grants, a $1.5 million investment over three years, to support campus expansion of services to underrepresented students. The board of trustees then took a request to the Minnesota legislature that resulted in a base investment of $11 million per year to improve the support of underrepresented students. Guided by the system office's student affairs area and the diversity and multiculturalism division, campus-based allocations of $7.4 million per year were distributed based upon student enrollment and percentage of diverse populations. In addition, a competitive grant program resulted in three Centers for Access and Oppor-

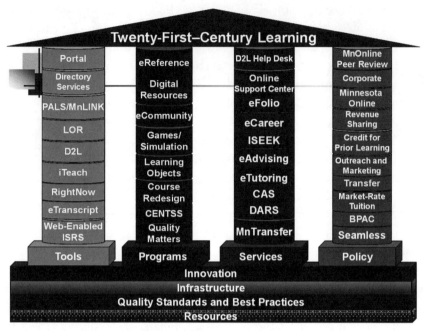

Figure 15.1 21st Century Learning

tunity funded at $3.4 million per year. These centers were developed as partnerships between colleges and universities and the school districts.

Using the best-in-class practices that promote student success, campuses now serve student populations in a much more targeted manner. Activities have included summer bridge programs, first-year experience or extended orientation, learning communities, intrusive advising, and supplemental instruction. Each of the system institutions participates in the Community College Student Survey on Engagement, commonly known as CCSSE, and the National Student Survey on Engagement to enable campuses to monitor student engagement. College teams participated in the Minnesota Student Engagement Institute, where information from the CCSSE was used to develop student success action plans for the year.

The outcomes were worthwhile. The enrollment of new underrepresented students increased 22 percent from fall 2008 to fall 2009 for the Minnesota State Colleges and Universities System. These groups included students of color, low-income students, and students whose parents did not attend college. More than 7,300 new underrepresented students enrolled, with 8,000 more underrepresented students returned to the system's institutions in fall 2009, a 15-percent increase over the previous year. The total number of underrepresented students in fall 2009 was 94,302, an increase of 18 percent. Additional student outcomes were noted: improved participation, retention, articulation to the next course, and improved GPAs. Some of the partnerships reflected work with state tribal schools and tribal colleges.

INNOVATION: ONLINE EDUCATION AND SERVICES

The Minnesota State Colleges and Universities System determined that online education was a major part of the future of higher education. Minnesota Online was created in 2002 upon the recommendation of a systemwide e-learning task force, which studied the distance-learning environment and sought ways to advance online learning by leveraging the resources of the system through collaboration. The purpose of Minnesota Online is to provide a collaborative framework for serving the online learners of the Minnesota State Colleges and Universities System.

Oversight of Minnesota Online is provided by the Minnesota Online Council, a unique systemwide entity comprising stakeholders from across the system with the purpose of assisting Minnesota Online to identify and initiate high-priority activities to advance online education in the system. The council is an advisory body.

Over the years, Minnesota Online has provided leadership to the campuses on the promotion and growth of online learning and has driven and supported innovation, including the following: the creation of eFolio; expediting the accreditation of online programs; the push for greater seamlessness of student support services; marketing of online programs in the system; and the operation of the Online Student Support Center as well as various student support services, including eTutoring, eLibrary services, and a network of student test proctoring.

Through this collaboration, the system has seen extraordinary growth in online enrollment over the past eight years with a headcount in online credit and noncredit courses growing from just over 16,900 in the 2003 fiscal year to 95,889 in 2010, a 469-percent increase. Online course sections expanded from 1,525 in 2003 to 8,775 in 2010, a 475-percent increase. Another major growth area was in online programs, which grew from 67 in 2003 to 328 in 2010, a 389-percent increase.

Minnesota Online currently is being guided by the system's Online Action Plan with the objectives of improving student access and increasing efficiency through collaboration. Actions currently being implemented address the improvement of course quality through the "Quality Matters" courses, assisting campuses in preparing faculty to teach online through a resource being developed in conjunction with our Center for Teaching and Learning, and the creation of a set of learning objects for use by the campuses to help prepare students for taking online courses.

INNOVATION: BUILDING A SEAMLESS SYSTEM

A key emphasis for the system is transferability. Prior to merger in 1994, the universities, community colleges, and the University of Minnesota faculty developed the Minnesota Transfer, MnTransfer, created to accomplish a general core around ten areas of curriculum. This enabled students to transfer the full associate of arts degree to state universities and to the University of Minnesota. The system continued to develop more transfer pathways with supported articulation councils. With the inclusion of the technical colleges after merger, major efforts were developed to determine agreed-upon mechanisms for technical college participation in the MnTransfer. This included the development of a new baccalaureate in applied sciences for the specific transfer to universities.

In order for the system to maximize the combined structure, five major strategies were developed in 2001 around making transfer work for students: the ongoing support of the MnTransfer curriculum, the support of articulation agreements required for program approval, the development of transfer specialists on each campus, the establishment of a transfer website with all pertinent information regarding transfer, and an appeals process for students who felt they did not receive an adequate review. In addition, the system invested in a statewide licensing for DARS (Degree Audit Reporting System) and CAS (Condition Acquisition and Reporting System). With the advent of more students attending more than one institution at a time, the system initiated a Business Practices Alignment Committee to review more than 120 policies and procedures to make more seamless educational experiences available to students.

One of the major changes was the system moving to a common start date and standardizing other processes and procedures for a more common look and feel to students. This work provided the foundation for the next generation of seamless policies and tools for students. The initiative is called Students First and focuses on the following services to students within the system: a single search/front-end tool, single application, course equivalency builder, single registration, grad planner, and single bill payment.

To recap the undertaking, more than 500,000 transfer credits were accepted from within the system, and another 539,000 were accepted from outside the system in 2008, with the number of transfer credits accepted increasing by 65 percent from 1999 to 2008. Ninety percent of transfer credits to state universities were accepted. New transfer students accounted for 24 percent of all new students in 2008. The number of new transfer students increased by 51 percent from 1999 to 2008. In keeping with continuous quality improvement, the college and university student associations joined with the academic and student affairs division to conduct a survey on transfer success in 2010. Several findings informed the ongoing improvement of transfer, that is, more information for students, a policy that supports course outlines being available for transfer decisions, and more information on the appeals process. A Smart Transfer Toolkit was developed as a result of the student survey information.

INNOVATION: ACCOUNTABILITY

Higher education will be held to increasingly high levels of accountability. The system developed an interactive dashboard to display the outcomes of all the campuses, colleges, and universities as collective groups and the system as a whole. (The dashboard summary is displayed in figure 15.2.) The accountability dashboard was launched in June 2008, with ten proposed measures of accountability. The measures aligned with the strategic directions and goal areas. Under the strategic direction for access and opportunity, the metric was a percent change in enrollment, tuition and fees, and persistence and completion rates. Still under development is a measure for transfer. For the strategic direction on high-quality programs and services, the metrics included licensure pass rates and student engagement. A measure still being developed is high-quality learning.

With economic competitiveness, the measure is related to the employment of graduates. Additional measures related to the financial viability direction include the facilities condition index and the composite financial index. Innovation required more qualitative reflection; at this point, campuses report innovations they are undertaking and their outcomes. The dashboard presents focused and easily understood information with trend lines over time, visual and tabular displays, and multiple levels of information with drill-down or cascading granularity. The key value is that the dashboard provides a tool to direct decision makers' at-

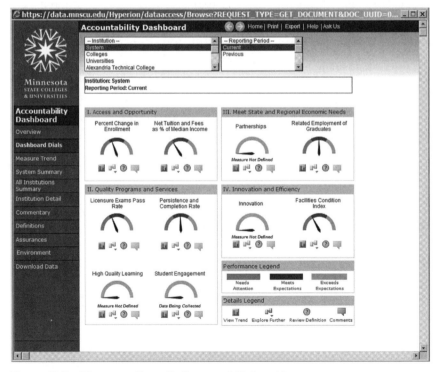

Figure 15.2   Minnesota State Colleges and Universities

tention to key issues. The dashboard allows for an assignment of value to the performance and a dial that indicates "meets expectation," "exceeds expectation," or "does not meet expectation." These levels were determined by national performance status, statewide status, or a level determined by the board of trustees.

This dashboard provides a transparent mechanism to review campus and system performance. The board of trustees chose to award performance pay to presidents based on the level of goal attainment. The next generation of accountability will include what the system has termed "action analytics." Based on business intelligence and the principles of predictive modeling, the Minnesota State Colleges and Universities System has begun to develop a robust system for analytics. Predictive modeling is the process by which a model is created or chosen to try to predict the probability of an outcome. Academic analytics combines large data sets, statistical techniques, and predictive modeling to produce "actionable intelligence." The system is now working on moving from the dashboard, which reflects reporting "after-the-fact" summative data to institutional-level actions that change outcomes.

We continue to pursue the next opportunities to improve access, opportunity, and success to our learners. We look to a better understanding of how analytics can be utilized in the reimagination of higher education postrecession and how these assessment and analytical tools can be used to improve student access, affordability, success, and financial sustainability. It is important to share that the Bill and Melinda Gates Foundation awarded the grant to pursue the development of a national agenda for action analytics with additional support by the Minnesota State Colleges and Universities Foundation. This included the establishment of an Action Analytics Education Partnership, with the Minnesota State Colleges and Universities System and Capella University being the founding members. A website has been developed to expand the national conversation and development of accountability and analytics capabilities.

INNOVATION: CREATING POWERFUL PARTNERSHIPS

The Minnesota State Colleges and Universities System is a case study in smart collaboration. Innovation consistently has been supported through powerful system partnerships that have emphasized new ways of getting things accomplished. Several campuses have structural combinations of community and technical colleges. Minnesota State Community and Technical College, Minnesota West Community and Technical College, the Northeast Higher Education District, Northland Community and Technical College, and others have multiple community sites. In addition, a unique colocation exists between a state university and a technical college. The system also claims one of the only state and tribally supported colleges, the Fond du Lac Tribal Community College. These structural combinations have provided innovative administration, shared services, and program and student service delivery as well as a very innovative distance Minnesota online consortium.

Partnerships also have been developed to create innovative collaborations between colleges and school districts. The Anoka Technical College Secondary Technical Education Program is a joint effort of the Anoka–Hennepin School District, the Minnesota State Colleges and Universities System, Anoka County, local business and industry partners, and students and parents in the community. It provides high school students with a seamless transition to the technical college; it is a premier example of how two different levels of education can work together. The focus has been both a hands-on technical education to applied learners and on how technical education stimulates economic growth. K–12 and higher education must work together toward a new focus on the learner. Institutions are responsible for a complete package of rigor and readiness—challenge and support—that prepares rural learners for successful careers in a global economy.

The system invested in a pilot for several rural colleges that worked together with local school districts to build a K–14 connection. The work resulted in a commitment to develop the following: a common calendar, a common student ID, enhanced career pathways, curriculum alignment for K–14, increased postsecondary enrollment options possibilities, new delivery models and technology, and work toward common faculty and teacher credentialing. Partnerships were the key ingredient with the Centers of Excellence in targeted industries: manufacturing, applied engineering, information technology security and health care. These centers have served as incubators of innovation for the system. They were based upon several criteria, including partnerships between colleges and universities and industry, K–12 schools, and communities, all to better deliver state-of-the-art curriculum in key state industries.

In 2005, the Minnesota State Legislature passed legislation and appropriated funding to create Centers of Excellence as part of the Minnesota State Colleges and University System. Each center was expected to become a regional or national leader within a specific area of education and training and exemplify the demonstration of strong ties to employers, a continuum of academic content, a variety of student-engagement strategies and entry points, and strong partnerships between four-year and two-year institutions. The authorizing legislation also specified that each center would be built upon strong existing programs, improved performance in related programs, strengthened quality and numbers of graduates, and integrated academic and training outcomes with business interests and opportunities.

The six goal areas established for the Centers of Excellence were new pathways for communication among all partners, including industry, education, and learners; identified industry opportunities and the related workforce preparation that these opportunities require; assistance for learners to discover and prepare for careers in center-aligned fields; stronger courses, programs, and learning opportunities through cross-campus activity; changes in the content and delivery of educational services; and revenue and leveraging of additional resources. These centers have evidenced the use of innovative strategies for engaging business and academic partners, as well as the successful implementation of new or enhanced methods for reaching students across a wide age spectrum.

INNOVATION: P–20 COMMITMENT

First established by the system's chancellor in April 2003, the Minnesota P–16 Education Partnership began as a voluntary collaboration among fifteen statewide P–12 schools and postsecondary organizations, systems, and agencies. These partners are committed to working to maximize the achievement of all P–16 students while promoting the efficient use of state resources, thereby helping the state realize the maximum value for its investment. The partnership provides a structure for ensuring consistent leadership that promotes the interests of all students, articulating an encompassing vision of education and working to turn that vision into reality. What sets this partnership apart from previous collaborations is its broad base, fully inclusive of both P–12 and higher education, and the commitment to a partnership of key educational leaders and policymakers who are willing to invest their time, energy, and resources in the ongoing operation of this project. The title of the group was changed to P–20 to embrace graduate education. At this time, the areas of work group discussion for the P–20 members are college and career readiness, STEM (Science, Technology, Engineering and Math) achievement gap strategy, and rigorous course-taking strategy.

INNOVATION: GRAD-U-ATE PROJECT

The Grad-U-ate Project for degree completion starts with baccalaureate completion (those with ninety-plus credits) and moves down to include completion of associate's degrees and high school diplomas. The idea is to allow students first to learn of the choices throughout the Minnesota State Colleges and Universities System and at the University of Minnesota and then see what works best for their goals and/or quickest routes to a degree. We have the advantage of u.Select as a "credit bank" and degree completion comparisons. Having more associate's-degree opportunities at state colleges and universities should only help students. If a student has the majority of associate's credits at a state university, it is much easier to complete the requirements there for that degree, including residency, rather than having to transfer and complete a few courses at a two-year college.

INNOVATION: LEADING VETERANS' PARTNERSHIPS

One very innovative facet of system leadership resulted from collaboration with the Minnesota National Guard as part of its reintegration program "Beyond the Yellow Ribbon." This statewide undertaking has put meaning and action behind the words and slogans to "Support Our Troops." The Minnesota State Colleges and Universities

System participates both with soldiers and with their families. System staff members make presentations at Family Preparation Academies to help prepare service members and families for deployments and at Family Readiness Academies prior to the soldiers' returns. Similar presentations, along with individualized advising and education information, are provided upon return at the soldiers' demobilization and at thirty-day, sixty-day, and sometimes one-year reintegration events sponsored by the National Guard.

During these events, soldiers have asked system presenters to help them receive credit for their military learning and to assist with their education and life planning. Working with the Minnesota Department of Veterans Affairs and National Guard partners, and with the support of a congressionally directed grant award administered through the Fund for the Improvement of Postsecondary Education, the system has developed two electronic innovations to answer these requests for help. The Veterans Education Transfer System translates a service member's military training to specific college majors. To begin this process, the system uses a series of national crosswalks to move from military occupational classifications to college majors using the credit recommendations of the American Council on Education. At this early stage, tracking is limited to technical education programs; in the future, it will be expanded to other majors.

Using the state-adopted degree audit system (DARS, u.Select) as the interfacing database and engine, a soldier is able to find occupational training related to her or his military training at a college where faculty already have reviewed the curriculum and awarded academic credit. Details of the major and the amount of credit available at any system university or college are presented online for the service member's or veteran's consideration prior to selection of a major or college. The Minnesota State Colleges and Universities System responded to the request for a career and education planning tool to accompany the credit transfer system. Through an internal partnership with the system's own Century College, the system created an electronic life-planning tool called GPS LifePlan (Goals + Plans = Success). This tool takes a holistic approach to life planning and is used in the classroom by faculty, by campus counselors with individual students, in small groups by individual students online, and now by members of the National Guard. In addition, the system contracts with the Department of Veterans Affairs to operate an information center called MyMilitaryEducation housed and operated on the Minnesota Online Help Center.

All these innovations occurred through the realization by these partners that none of us can do what all of us can do. The partnerships are the means to accomplish these ends. More important, they inspire the innovation that comes from viewing the same problem from multiple perspectives.

INNOVATION: NATIONAL-LEVEL PARTICIPATION

The system joined Indiana and Utah in a Lumina-supported initiative to develop a "tuning process" comparable to the Bologna Process in Europe. Faculty from two disciplines, graphic design and biology; from the system campuses; private colleges; and the University of Minnesota explored more seamless curricular pathways. Statewide discipline meetings now will be hosted in the areas to encourage further dialogue among the faculty members in the disciplines. In 2007, the system heads of nearly two dozen public postsecondary systems created the Access to Success Initiative to pursue two goals: increase the number of college-educated adults in their respective states and ensure that their institutions' graduates included more young people from low-income and minority families by 2015. They did so because they recognized that a college education—now more than ever—is the surest route to a decent job and contributes to the health of our democracy.

By 2015, the National Association of System Heads (NASH) members who signed on to the project have pledged that their systems will halve the gaps in college going and college success that separate African American, Latino, and American Indian students from white and Asian American students and low-income students from more affluent students. Most higher education funding models have at the core student enrollment and program costs. The Minnesota State Colleges and Universities System is no exception. Systems are looking at such outcome measures as graduation and allocating some funds to meet those measures. Discussions have been concerned with whether some portion of our allocation should be focused more directly on "results" and what results or outcomes might be used toward completion.

While success as measured by graduation might be the end result, it is at the end of a process that is at least two to six years long. Believing that there are several points along the way to successful completion that should be considered, the Minnesota State Colleges and Universities System joined with six other systems in an initiative sponsored by NASH called "early indicators of student success." The intent of the project was to look at "momentum points" along the path from matriculation to graduation that either help or hinder a student's likelihood of success. From indicators identified in a literature review and analyses by the Institute for Higher Education Leadership Policy, the following indicators were selected: completion of developmental education, completion of gateway courses in math and English, first-year credit accumulation, first-year completion ratio of credits completed to credits attempted, earned summer credits, full-time enrollment, and continuous enrollment.

Staff in the system office did an analysis of these factors. Results are still preliminary, but a relationship between several of these factors and eventual success was found. Additional analysis and expansion to more cohorts are planned. Based on the limited work that was completed, however, we may explore which one to three of these might be incorporated into the allocation formula. The future will require more emphasis on decreasing the achievement gap among underserved students; improving college and work readiness, recruitment, and retention; and successful completion for students. It will require higher education to find even better models to deliver higher education in more affordable ways. And it will require that we fuse training and learning with workforce and careers.

INNOVATION: LEADERSHIP

There is little that can be labeled as "innovative" in the world of governance these days, but the work of a higher education system can unfold as a process of inclusion or exclusion. Bringing everyone together in an environment that permits the best yields in creativity, cooperation, and public service care is the "magic" in good governance. For the Minnesota State Colleges and Universities System, the leadership team has coalesced to shape an innovative and students-first community. Even with the presence of technological advances, the old-school need for eye contact and face-to-face interaction remains an important part of the governance structure for the system. The presidents of thirty-two institutions, the seven universities, and the twenty-six two-year colleges come together with the system office senior team monthly to discuss systemwide issues and any matter that is slated for governing board information or action.

Why does this governance model, the Leadership Council, work for Minnesota? The following are examples of success for the Leadership Council:

- Continuing communication emerges as a key part of the community. It builds trust.
- The presidents and staff are empowered. They work on behalf of each other and the system.
- Mutual regard and support between and among the colleges and universities occur. Team building becomes a natural focus.
- Competition among and between the sectors is diminished. Campus CEOs are collegial, save for student athletic rivalries.
- System actions are discussed before consideration by the governing board. The rule of "no surprises" makes everyone equal.
- The ability for presidents to have a voice about all system policies is essential. It reduces what can be called "power paranoia."
- The structure produces a better, stronger, and preshopped product for all users. It is a tested method or direction.
- The council is the ideal means to channel opinions. The interaction demonstrates by action, words, and deeds that the broad views of leadership are respected.

Is the concept and practice original for higher education? Probably not, but its real use and outcomes support intelligent, productive, creative, bold, and sometimes courageous leaders. Without this, any level of innovation in any other area of endeavor just will not work.

MOVING TO THE NEXT LEVEL OF INNOVATION: BUILDING A ROADMAP FOR TWENTY-FIRST-CENTURY LEARNING

Today, work is underway on the integration of customized learning experiences, assessment-based learning outcomes, wikis, blogs, social networking, and mobile learning. In addition, full access to data and predictive modeling opportunities are being explored to improve and customize student learning for success. In partnership with the University of Minnesota and the Minnesota Department of Education, we have developed the Minnesota Learning Commons. Student access and opportunity without success are not enough. Each student needs to have an educational pathway for meeting work and career expectations. The system cofounded the Center for Transforming Student Services with Western Cooperative for Educational Telecommunications; it provides educational institutions with the tools and training they need to develop and deliver high-quality student services online. Effectively implemented student services are a crucial component of student retention, engagement, and satisfaction. Through CENTSS (Center to Transform Student Services), institutions are able to blend the power of technology with the personal attention of traditional support services.

Several tools have been developed to enable students to improve their toolkit for success. These tools include the efolio, efolio for Veterans, GPS Life Plan, and ISEEK, a multieducational and cross-agency partnership to program an Internet system for education and employment knowledge. The Learning Commons provides a statewide learning object repository for P–20 learning needs. It is designed to provide access to effective and efficient online learning provided by Minnesota public education partners. The Commons is a P–16 gateway to many collaborative platforms, including access to online courses and programs; digital resources and tools; teacher and staff training; online support for students, educators, parents, and citizens of Minnesota; joint course and service development and sharing; showcasing best practices; and group licensing.

FINAL WORD

It is worth sharing an observation from the popular *Shift Happens* that swept the Internet several years ago: "We are currently preparing students for jobs that don't exist, using technologies that haven't been invented, in order to solve problems we don't even know are problems yet." Innovation is a characteristic in higher education leadership that is crucial for advancement at all levels.

BIBLIOGRAPHY

Academic Quality Improvement Program. *Principles and Categories for Improving Academic Quality.* Rev. ed. Chicago: Higher Learning Commission, 2008.

Anderson, Edward, and Donald O. Clifton. *StrengthsQuest: Discover and Develop Your Talents in Academics, Career and Beyond.* Princeton: The Gallup Organization, 2002.

Aronowitz, Stanley, and Henry A. Giroux. *Postmodern Education, Politics, Culture, and Social Criticism.* Minneapolis: University of Minnesota Press, 1991.

Brint, Steven G., and Jerome Karabel. *The Diverted Dream: Community Colleges and the Promise of Educational Opportunity in America, 1900–1985.* New York: Oxford University Press, 1989.

Browning, Robert, and Edward Johnston. *Men and Women/Robert Browning.* London: Doves Press, 1908.

The Carnegie Foundation for the Advancement of Teaching. *Quality and Equality: New Levels of Federal Responsibility for Higher Education: A Special Report and Recommendations by the Commission.* New York: McGraw-Hill, 1968.

Carnevale, Anthony P., and Donna M. Desrochers. "The Missing Middle: Aligning Education and the Knowledge Economy" (April 2002). Available online at www.ed.gov/about/offices/list/ovae/pi/hs/carnevale.doc (accessed November 20, 2010).

Cerbo, Toni, and Kerri Mercer. *Personal Assessment of the College Environment (PACE)* (December 2009). Available online at www.grcc.edu/files/ddevries/GRCC_PACEreport_2009_final.pdf (accessed August 22, 2011).

Chickering, Arthur W., and Zelda F. Gamson. "The Seven Principles for Good Practice in Undergraduate Education" (March 1987). *American Association for Higher Education and Accreditation Bulletin.* Available online at www.aahea.org/bulletins/articles/sevenprinciples1987.htm (accessed August 22, 2011).

Christensen, Clayton M., Michael B. Horn, and Curtis W. Johnson. *Disrupting Class: How Disruptive Innovation Will Change the Way the World Learns.* New York: McGraw-Hill, 2008.

Collins, Jim. *Good to Great: Why Some Companies Make the Leap and Others Don't.* New York: HarperCollins, 2001.

Cortes, Carlos E. "The Societal Curriculum and the School Curriculum: Allies or Antagonists?" *Educational Leadership* 36, no. 7 (1979): 475–79.

Dao, James, and Shanker, Thom. "No Longer a Soldier, Shinseki Has a New Mission" (November 10, 2009). *New York Times.* Available online at www.nytimes.com/2009/11/11/us/politics/11vets.html?pagewanted=all (accessed August 22, 2009).

Davis, James W., and Kenneth M. Dolbeare. *Little Groups of Neighbors: The Selective Service System.* Chicago: Markham, 1968.

Delpit, Lisa. *Other People's Children: Cultural Conflict in the Classroom.* New York: New Press, 2005.

Disney Institute. *Be Our Guest: Perfecting the Art of Customer Service.* New York: Disney Enterprises, 2001.

Drucker, Peter F. *The Daily Drucker: 366 Days of Insight and Motivation for Getting the Right Things Done.* New York: HarperBusiness, 2004.

Gelb, Michael J., and Sarah Miller Caldicott. *Innovate Like Edison: The Five-Step System for Breakthrough Business Success.* New York: Plume, 2008.

Gladwell, Malcolm. *The Tipping Point: How Little Things Can Make a Big Difference.* Boston: Little, Brown, 2000.

Giroux, Henry A. *Pedagogy and the Politics of Hope: Theory, Culture, and Schooling.* Boulder, CO: Westview/Harper Collins, 1997.

Godin, Seth. *Tribes: We Need You to Lead Us.* New York: Portfolio, 2008.

Hefferlin, J. B. Lon. *Dynamics of Academic Reform.* 1st ed. San Francisco: Jossey-Bass, 1969.

Higher Education: The Lessons of Experience. Washington, DC: World Bank, 1994.

Juhnke, Ralph. "The National Community College Benchmark Project." *New Directions for Community Colleges,* no. 134 (2006): 67–72.

Kelly, Tom, with Jonathan Littman. *The Art of Innovation: Lessons in Creativity from IDEO.* New York: Doubleday, 2001.

Landsberger, Henry A. *Hawthorne Revisited: Management and the Worker: Its Critics, and Developments in Human Relations in Industry.* Ithaca, NY: Cornell University, 1955.

Michigan Tech's Environmental Sustainability Committee. *Greenprint for Environmental Sustainability in Campus Operations and Activities* (July 2001). Available online at www.esc.mtu.edu (accessed July 2010).

The National Center for Public Policy and Higher Education. *Measuring Up 2006.* (December 31, 2006). Available online at http://measuringup .highereducation.org/nationalpicture/nationalpdfspresentations.cfm eg. (accessed March 2011).

The National Commission on Excellence in Education. *A Nation at Risk: The Imperative for Education Reform* (April 1983). Available online at www2 .ed.gov/pubs/NatAtRisk/index.html (accessed November 20, 2010).

O'Banion, Terry, and Laura Weidner. "The Nature of Innovation in the Community College." *Leadership Abstracts* 22, no. 12 (December 2009). Available online at http://www.league.org/blog/post.cfm/the-nature-of-innovation (accessed May 29, 2011).

Pink, Daniel H. *Drive: The Surprising Truth about What Motivates Us.* New York: Riverhead Books, 2009.

"Principles of High Performance Organizations" (2010). *Academic Quality Improvement Program, The Higher Learning Commission.* Available online at www.ncahlc.org/download/annualmeeting/10Handouts/SpangehlA-SAT-0845-a.pdf (accessed August 22, 2011).

Project on Redefining the Meaning and Purpose of Baccalaureate Degrees. *Integrity in the College Curriculum: A Report to the Academic Community: The Findings and Recommendations of the Project on Redefining the Meaning and Purpose of Baccalaureate Degrees.* Washington, DC: Association of American Colleges, 1985.

Ravitch, Diane. *The Death and Life of the Great American School System: How Testing and Choice Are Undermining Education.* New York: Basic Books, 2010.

Rogers, Everett M. *Diffusion of Innovations.* 4th ed. New York: Free Press, 1995.

Schumpeter, Joseph. *The Theory of Economic Development.* Boston: Harvard University Press, 1934.

Senge, Peter M. *The Fifth Discipline: The Art and Practice of the Learning Organization.* New York: Doubleday-Dell, 1990.

Snyder, Thomas D., Sally A. Dillow, and Charlene M. Hoffman. "3." In *Digest of Education Statistics 2008.* Washington, DC: National Center for Education Statistics, Institute of Education Sciences, 2009.

Spellings, Margaret. *A Test of Leadership Charting the Future of U.S. Higher Education*. Washington, DC: U.S. Department of Education, 2006.

Spendolini, Michael. *The Benchmarking Book*. New York: Amacom, 1992.

Watson, Gregory H. *Strategic Benchmarking Reloaded with Six Sigma*. New York: John Wiley and Sons, 2007.

West, Michael A., and James L. Farr. *Innovation and Creativity at Work: Psychological and Organizational Strategies*. Chichester, UK: Wiley, 1990.

INDEX

Page numbers of figures (tables, charts, etc.) are italicized.

Ward, David, 24
Washburn University, 127
Watson, Russell J., 155–58
Weber, Dave, 77–80
Weidner, Laura, 57–59, 63
Welch, Jack, 4
We Need You to Lead Us (Godin), 66
West, Michael A., xii

Western Association of Schools and
    Colleges, 28, 32
Western Technical College, 97–99
working adults, 102–3, 136
work-study, 124, 136–37
World Bank, 96
World War I, 5
World War II, 6–8, 13, 31

ABOUT THE EDITORS

Senior Volume Editor: Allan M. Hoffman

Allan M. Hoffman is an experienced educator and human services administrator. He has held executive-level positions in all sectors of American higher education, including a public doctoral research-level university, comprehensive state university, comprehensive community college, private academic health sciences center, and multicampus private university, as well as a health care delivery organization. He served as president of the Santa Barbara Graduate Institute, a TCS-Education System affiliate. He has served as president, CEO, vice president, dean, executive officer, and faculty member. He was on the design team for the Academic Quality Improvement Program (AQIP) of the Higher Learning Commission, which is an alternative accreditation process for institutions pursuing systematic continuous quality improvements.

Dr. Hoffman has published on key issues in higher education leadership and focused on innovations within higher education and total quality improvement. He has provided consulting services to schools, colleges, and business organizations in multinational settings. Dr. Hoffman, the recipient of numerous awards, has served as a coach and mentor for higher educational leaders interested in developing innovative and entrepreneurial projects and programs. Several of his books are utilized as texts in leadership programs in higher education. He earned his B.S. magna cum laude from the University of Hartford and received two M.A. degrees and an Ed.D. from Teachers College, Columbia University, where he was named a Kellogg Fellow.

Stephen D. Spangehl is vice president for accreditation relations at the Higher Learning Commission. He created the AQIP in 1999 when the commission's grant proposal for the development of an alternative reaccreditation process based on quality improvement principles was funded by the Pew Charitable Trusts. He has directed AQIP from its beginning through its growth to its present size with two hundred participating institutions. From 1991 to 1999, he served as a staff member with responsibility for coordinating commission services to more than 250 institutions. Spangehl's prior experience in higher education includes more than twenty years in both faculty and administrative roles from developmental education to academic affairs. Specializing in linguistics and medieval literature, he earned his B.A. and M.A. degrees from New York University and his Ph.D. from the University of Pennsylvania.

He has served since as a member of the Malcolm Baldrige National Quality Award Program's board of examiners, on the education and training board of the American Society for Quality, and on the board of the National Consortium for Continuous Improvement. An activist for the incorporation of systems theory and continuous improvement ideas and techniques in higher education, he has written and spoken widely on leadership, innovation, assessment, general and developmental education, and other current topics.